VALUE-ADDED ATTITUDE & ACTION

William I. Gorden

VALUE-ADDED
Attitude And Action

Copyright © 1995 William I. Gorden

Library Of Congress Catalog
Card Number 94-96463

ISBN 0-9643860-1-1

Printed in the United States of America

All rights reserved. No part of this book may be reproduced or transmitted in any form or by any means, electronic or mechanical, including photocopy, recording, or any information storage and retrieval system, without permission in writing from the publisher.

Production Editing: Capenhurst Publishing
Cover Design: Daniel V. West
Printing and Binding: Fairway Press, Lima, Ohio
Published by WEGO BOOKS, Kent, Ohio 44240

♦ TABLE OF CONTENTS ♦

Acknowledgements iv
Preface v

Chapter 1 - THE FAMILY CONNECTION

Beyond Closeness To Connectedness 2
Harry Was A Family Man 2
Call Me Walt 6
The Dream Sidetracked 8
The Unfriendly Workplace 9
Feeling Like A Number 11

Chapter 2 - OUR STORY

A Rough Start 14
A Slippery Mystery Solved 15
From Adversity To Diversity 16
To Be Known By Name 24
Family Produces Added Value 25

Chapter 3 - COMMUNICATION AT WORK

Hi Hon, Can You Come Here? 28
There Is No Morale Problem Here 30
Communication Is More Than Information 32
Conflict Goes With The Job 33
Bosses From Hell 35
Talking As Though Walking On Eggs 36
Communication Rich 37
What Do Employees Need To Know? 38
Two-Way And Frequent 39

Chapter 4 - WORK HOARSE vs. CLEAR VOICE

Success Depends Upon Undistorted Information . . . 42
Bootlicking Hurts Employee Voice 42
Workers' Range Of Voice 43
Anti-Union, Anti-Voice 44
The Voice Of Partnership 46
Critical Involvement 48
Voiceless 50

Chapter 5 - WE WILL NOT GIVE QUALITY...

What The Customer Wants 54
Three God-Words 54
Cut The Slogans 55
The Quality Movement 56
The Ongoing Improvement Process 58
TQM As Service 60
Benchmarking & Going For The Gold 62

Chapter 6 - CLOSE TO THE CUSTOMER

Everyone Is A Customer 66
A Leaky Bureaucracy 67
Suppliers And Customers 69
Most Favored Customer Status 71

Chapter 7 - T.E.A.M.

Teams Are Partnerships 76
Many Different Varieties 78
In Different Configurations 79
Not All Harmony And Song 80

Team Problem Solving 81
The Rules Of Teamwork 83

Chapter 8 - SERVICE ENHANCEMENT

This Place Is A Zoo 90
Getting Closer To The Public 91
Confidence Is Earned 93
50,000 Moments Of Truth 94

Chapter 9 - THE NEXT CHAPTER

Why Not A Circus? 98
If Not A Circus, Why Not Butterflies? 103

NOTES AND REFERENCES

References 106
List Of Companies Researched/Consulted 111
About The Author 112

Acknowledgements

Value-Added Attitude and Action would not have been possible without the help of many individuals who took me into their places of work like an old friend. A selected list of those companies and organizations is included on page 111. Several individuals, who arranged on-site interviews, merit special mention: Gerald Sargent, now with Challenger, Gray and Christmas in Houston, scheduled interviews for me in Dallas; Jack White, with HELP Bronx, smoothed entry into organizations in Washington D.C.; and John Izzo, with Einstein Consulting, did the same San Diego. I wish to thank Neal Irwin, Ronda Smith, Rogers Slease, and Wayne Wogan for their attention to detail and thoughtful comments after reading drafts of this manuscript. Finally, I express my appreciation to Dan West for preparing this text for the printer.

Preface:
Proceed Directly To Goal

My goal for <u>Value-Added Attitude and Action</u> is to add value to those lives I touch. More particularly, I want to increase understanding and adoption of attitudes and actions that enrich the workplace and working lives.

Value-added attitude and action is no simple matter. Rather it is a complex process in which human energies, competencies, and good will are coordinated to transform goods and services into what is of special value to users. The good news is that value-added attitude and action when present in a few in our places of work will become positively contagious.

Motivational slogans and work ethic are insufficient for transforming today's corporate environment. I argue there are certain **must** conditions for making the workplace a value-added place:

- work **must** have meaning to head and heart,
- vision and initiative **must** be widely present,
- managers **must** have business savvy,
- superiors **must** earn loyalty by sharing decisions,
- employees' well-being **must** equal other stakeholders,
- money and benefits **must** be fairly distributed,
- the work culture **must** engender connectedness,

- communication **must** be rich and voice must be valued,
- quality improvement **must** be foremost and continuous,
- customer relations **must** be governed by good will,
- suppliers and customers **must** treat each other as partners.

When these **musts** are met--when value-added attitude and action are organization-wide, from the security guard at the gate to the chief executive officer--America can better compete in the race for world class quality.

My message is practical. I am committed to those well-conceived efforts to improve quality. Corporate continuous quality improvement efforts, however, often are misdirected because they are too much profit-driven. This is not to suggest that profit is unimportant. I am not naive. But defining value-added only in terms of the bottom line squelches the best that is in us, that insatiable hunger and thirst for the good, the true and the beautiful. We are a people who want to do good while doing well. We want our work to add to the well-being of customers and to a safe environment.

My core message is expressed in the idea that each of us wants to make a difference--that we want to add value to what we do. I examine workplace conditions--the conectedness, commitment to quality, and the importance of employee voice--that affect worker attitude and commitment. Throughout I make observations of what companies are doing to improve quality and to please customers.

Q. Who should read <u>Value-Added Attitude and Action</u>?

A. This book is for all people who want to do more than earn a living.

Perhaps the readers that will benefit the most are those who have lived long enough to know that they can not expect a smile on the face of a waitress whose shoes pinch her feet or whose boss rarely says thanks. By that, I mean that this is a book for ordinary people who work hard in less than exciting jobs and who often are expected to do quality work in spite of personal difficulties, a poor work climate, and low pay. <u>Value-Added</u> also should have special benefit for those who know how important is the bottom line, who must meet payrolls, and whose attitude and action do much to shape the work environment.

Those few individuals who think that they are destined to boss while others are doomed to drudge work will find little comfort in <u>Value-Added</u>. Whoever you are, whether in various levels of management, a union member, non-union worker, or a temporary hire, you will discover that some of the positions I take will provoke argument.

Most people don't read a Preface. If you have read this far, it is a sign that you like to consult a road map before you begin a journey. That now is done. So proceed directly to Chapter One. You will find there and in the chapters that follow inspirational stories and experiences that have shaped my own and others' lives, and that can transform the workplace.

Please tell me if what you read rings true. I will appreciate hearing from you.

>Bill Gorden
P.O. Box 84, Kent, OH 44240

THE FAMILY CONNECTION

CHAPTER ONE

BEYOND CLOSENESS TO CONNECTEDNESS

"As a child is connected to the parent, to be connected with another person is the only security we ever have in life. In that sense, we never grow up."
--*Susan Johnson & Hara Estroff Marano*

Physical closeness between a mother and child serves the survival of the infant. Attachment to a responsible caregiver is the most basic of all rules of life. That need for **connectedness** is something we never lose. It is a primary motivation. The meaning of life and our mental health are entwined in bonding and connections with others. This principle not only applies to the family but to the workplace.

Harry Was A Family Man

Sometimes we can better appreciate the importance of connectedness by seeing it demonstrated in the lives of those who attain celebrity status. Harry's life is a love story. He was "his mother's son." Yet from his father, who was small in stature, he acquired a feistiness, courage, honesty, a veneration for women, and hunger to get rich. His father's speculation into wheat futures put him deeply in debt, a debt carried by Harry long after his father's death.

Debt put college out of the question for him. Rather he got a down-to-earth education in such jobs as a construction time keeper for the Santa Fe. He worked 10 hours a day, six days a week, and lived with railroad gangs in their tents. Later, he worked as a clerk in the basement of Kansas City's National Bank of Commerce, and then on his uncle's 600 acre farm. Everyone in the family worked to survive on the farm. To be a good farmer was something to take pride in.

One day, while visiting friends in Independence, he returned a cake plate to the Gates' house. It was there that Harry met the Gates' granddaughter, Bessie Wallace. He talked with her for two hours. Later he was invited to dinner, and after dinner he played the piano. He had earned a standing invitation to Sunday dinner. It was the beginning of letter after letter, hundreds of them, in which he poured out his heart to her. Bess and Harry were not married until she was 34 and he 35.

His letters were not mushy and romantic, nor was his proposal by mail. Only occasionally did one speak of love such as "I really never had any desire to make love to a girl just for the fun of it, and you have always been the reason." Many letters told of the mundane work on the farm such as putting hundreds of rings in hogs' noses. Some told of his religious convictions because he knew that was important to her, "I think there's more in acting than in talking," and, although a Baptist, he accepted her invitation to attend an Episcopal service.

At her suggestion, he read books by Charles Dickens, and he boasted of reading Plato's <u>Republic</u> rather than only magazines such as <u>Adventure</u> and <u>Everybody's Life</u>. Writing about breaking his leg, he commented, had taught him sympathy for others. He also confessed his less than masculine behavior of yelling when he had a tooth pulled, and expressed a distaste for guns when he wrote about his stint with the National Guard.

Several years later, yet before they were married, he would write from Europe of his leadership as Captain of the artillery "Wild Irish" Battery D. He enlisted his 5'8" 150 pound frame to fight the Germans in World War I. His dependence upon spectacles was so great that he took seven pairs with him. Early on he made it clear to his men that they had "to get along with me" and that he would bust any who would not. But he earned the respect of his "Wild Irish" recruits and made friends, some who many years later were important to him politically.

Harry did everything possible to persuade Bess to have a favorable opinion of him: he built a tennis court on the farm, bought an expensive automobile in order to make the trip from the farm to Independence more quickly, escorted her to the theater, and got into risky business ventures in hopes of making himself better able to support her.

His investments in a zinc mine failed. Selling oil leases failed. His partnership in a retail men's furnishings store failed. With several others, he took over a bank that he learned too late was tottering. No sooner had he sold it than it too failed. Not long after that he was cheated in a savings and loan stock selling venture. There was something persistent about him. If one thing failed, it was not long before he would begin another.

Other than his leadership role in the war, it was not until he ventured into politics that he would do well: first winning an election as a county commissioner whose major task was to keep the roads in good shape; then from 1927 to 1935, he served as presiding judge in Independence-Kansas City, Missouri. His oversight of roads was enlarged to arrange construction of many projects, including a new courthouse for Kansas City. And Harry ran a tight ship, clear of scandal in a town in which the Pendergasts' machine dictated politics.

On Sundays, Harry, Bess, and their daughter Margaret would drive to the farm for a midday fried chicken dinner. Harry's heart now included Bess, their daughter, and Mamma. He was responsible in all things. His car had to be clean and its tires carry the right pressure. He dressed carefully, and never went out the door without his hat, a hat he wore straight on his head.

Some years later after being elected to the Senate, his Special Committee to Investigate the National Defense was relentless in its efforts to rectify what he called "Santa Claus passes" to contractors. But he wrote Bess, who at that time was back in Missouri, "I hope I don't make any mistakes . . . Hope I won't be here too long."

And as president, Harry--the buck stops here--Truman will be remembered not only as "Give 'em hell, Harry", but also as a man terribly protective of his family. Remember his scathing letter to a critic who had reviewed his daughter Margaret's concert? "Some day I hope to meet you. When that happens you'll need a new nose, a lot of beefsteak for black eyes, and perhaps a supporter below."

> ## *ATTITUDE & ACTION*
>
> The most used metaphor to describe the workplace at its best is **family**. That was the theme song of the Pittsburgh Pirates when they won the world series in 1979. The message of the hit song "We Are Family" by Sister Sledge caught the imagination of the whole city.

Call Me Walt

The history of Disney echoes with two themes: Disney is **drama** and Disney is **family**. Disney as drama is evident in the concept that everyone is a part of the show--that all employees are members of a cast who act out their roles on stage. Disneyland is designed as an escape from the real world in which paying customers are guests of the happiest place on earth. Dress codes are seen as costuming. There are special ways to look, talk, and behave according to the role you play. The drama is carefully scripted.

A Disney training seminar is designed for employees to catch a bit of the same stardust they are expected to sprinkle upon those who enter Disneyland.

In its early days, Disney was known as a **first name friendly place to work** and a place where teamwork was essential. Walt Disney insisted that everyone call him "Walt." The stories that employees tell depict him as a family man, who reserved Saturdays for his daughters and as one who created Disneyland to provide his own and others' families a safe, clean, fun place to go.

A colleague research team from California, Ruth Smith and Eric Eisenberg, learned that Disney employees uncritically adopted the family atmosphere created for paying customers as the way Disney employees should be treated and should behave.

A ride operator they interviewed said, "These people are like my brothers and sisters." Another employee described his work relationships as "close knit" and "better than marriage." Yet another stated, "The people who work here treat each other as a family . . . We're a family presenting family entertainment, it's like inviting someone to our home to entertain them." Management encouraged this family-feeling by naming the annual party the "family picnic."

The Dream Sidetracked

As Disney expanded, management became more concerned about the bottom-line and profits. In the mid-80s, wages and benefits were cut for some hourly employees. Employees were shocked. They complained about how it used to be "Try to make the employees happy as possible so that they make the public happy" and now it's "let's save as much money as we can and make a buck."

Employees felt that they were no longer treated as family. Their talk was different: "It's just totally business," "They don't care," "It's not fun to work at Disneyland any more," and "Walt wanted family, but it's business now, not Walt's dream, that's shot, it's not what he wanted."

A 22-day strike disrupted Disneyland. The strike created a new drama at the gates of the Magic Kingdom--pickets, restraining orders, ultimatums of return to work or else, letters of replacement, hiring of replacements, and some employees crossing the picket line. And then the strikers came up with a tactic that hit management where it hurt--they paid to enter Disneyland and once inside distributed handbills to the public and told how disheartened they were because they no longer were treated as family. Shortly after that tactic, the strike was settled.

But relations between those who manned and had crossed picket lines and between labor and management were changed. A two-tier pay scale which was part of the strike settlement favored those with three or more years. Many hourly employees saw management as adversaries; they saw themselves as the "less wanted step-children."

In the years that have followed, Disney continues to promote its theme of the happiest place on earth, and has regained among many of its permanent employees the belief that Disney is a good place to work. Bright and talented young people apply in droves to work in Disney parks despite the long hours and modest wages. However, behind the scenes there are others far from excited about their jobs, such as the banks of telephone operators who know the tedium year after year of making reservations.

The Unfriendly Workplace

The opposite of connectedness, of course, is disconnectedness and alienation. The scourge of killings and grievous injuries by alienated Post Office employees and discharged workers are grim evidence of how vital is the human need to be a valued member in a workplace. The 1,000 killings each year within U.S. workplaces are not just the work of madmen who blow away anyone in their path; they are often lonely people, jilted lovers, mistreated employees driven to kill in revenge and then take their own lives. Life can become quite desperate when we invest years in a workplace yet feel unappreciated, unfulfilled, and unloved.

Efficient scheduling of work around the clock for hundreds and sometimes thousands of employees is no easy task for managers. Some work has to be performed at inconvenient times. Employees are expected to arrange their lives accordingly. Becuase Federal Express does much of its work at night, the company fired Diane Mutchler, one of its agents in Pittsburgh who failed to report for a night assignment. Ms. Mutchler was a single mother of three small children who could not find child care at night. "We Are Family" was not a song sung that week in Pittsburgh.

Companies are finding it costs less to pay overtime than to hire more employees. But that

> ## *ATTITUDE & ACTION*
>
> The intoxicating start-up of one's own business and the demands of making it grow can suck the oxygen out of your life, says Todd Logan, founder of Sportscape Inc. Publications in Winnetka, Illinois. Foremost of the signs that one is trapped and prisoner of one's own success, Todd declares, is **despair over the loss of closeness in important personal relationships**--"a breakdown in the relationships we value most."
>
> *--from Todd Logan's Mind of the Manager: Trapped in INC.*

strategy can be pushed only so far. The Flint, Michigan General Motors plant was struck to protest mandatory overtime that sometimes resulted in 66 hour workweeks and the suspension of several workers who refused to work an overtime shift. Allegheny Ludlum steel plants were struck after some workers were required to work 146 hours in two weeks. What do these unfortunate instances tell us? They warn us that workers have lives and families who need them in person and not just their paychecks. They also remind us that employees want family-friendly employers that negotiate rather than mandate work assignments, employers that help arrange child care, and employers that help employees nurture family.

Feeling Like A Number

Disconnectedness is the product of an urban landscape in which our identity is an ID number, and where, unlike in Cheers, only a few people know your name. Our hometown is not a place where we live, but some place where we grew up. Most of us work for organizations that are very big and in which it is easy to get lost. Our immediate family may be even more treasured as an enterprise grows large. It is ironic that creating a family-friendly work culture within our large work organizations is keenly valued, yet quite difficult to achieve.

Secretary of Labor Robert Reich has warned that the American middle class is splintering into three groups: an *underclass*, an *overclass*, and the largest group is an *anxious class*. The underclass is trapped in poverty and the inner cities. Overclass families are the well-educated and have moved to the suburbs, some which are protected by gates. They have prospered while the less-well educated have suffered a steep decline in living standards.

The anxious class, most of them in houses and apartments too small for their families, need two or three paychecks to deliver the standard of living that one used to supply. The forces that pull America apart work to the disadvantage of us all. Our national connectedness and competitive advantage, as Reich argues, hinge upon renewing "the compact among American business, American government, and American working men and women." Government must invest in infrastructure and, along with business, must invest in workers--in creating a skilled and flexible workforce and that also must mean creating a family-friendly workplace.

OUR STORY

CHAPTER TWO

A Rough Start

To augment our understanding of corporate America, several years ago I made a collection of company histories. Most of those histories began with accounts of the struggle and sacrifice of company founders. The best stories told of the sense of family that those early days had, and of the many ways companies are nurturing working relationships.

As with Disney, I studied the history of 3M. My

ATTITUDE & ACTION

Under CEO Livio DeSimone, 3M has slashed the time it takes to introduce new products in half. Two of his Commandments for managing creative people with his comments are:

Create a culture of cooperation.
"We should have as many people from as many disciplines as possible talking to each other."

Make the company a lifetime career.
Questioning managers who have had to cut their forces deeply, DeSimone asks, "Why did you get into a position that you had to lay off a bunch of people? How come you're so smart now?" 3M rarely lays off people.

contacts with this company began in the mid 70s. I learned how Minnesota Mining and Manufacturing started in 1902 because of the discovery of corundum on the north shore of Lake Superior. Next to diamonds, at that time, corundum was the hardest pure mineral known to the world. So the founders of 3M began as a company that mined and supplied abrasives to manufacturers. They were heavily into sandpaper manufacturing before they found that the corundum discovered was of inferior quality.

These were times when 3M stock was traded in Duluth bars at the rate of two shares for one shot. Rather than give up, they found suppliers of a better grade of corundum and other abrasive materials. However, learning to make sandpaper with abrasives that stuck was still more art than science.

A Slippery Mystery Solved

At one point, variations in the quality of their sandpaper was 1,000%; some stuck very well, in other cases the crushed minerals fell off before the glue dried. As the story goes, weeks went by as rejects mounted, until one day a workman noticed an oily film on water standing in a scrub pail. At the bottom of the pail was a small amount of crushed garnet that had been mopped up from the floor by a maintenance worker. Could it be that oil was somehow mixed with the abrasives?

Sleuthing discovered that the garnet had come by boat in a shipment from Spain. The Spanish steamer also had carried a large cargo of olive oil. During a storm, some of the casks of oil had broken open and leaked into the sacks of garnet.

They had 200 tons of oil-soaked garnet, and could not afford to simply discard it. After months of experimentation, a research-inclined superintendent found that washing the mineral and heating the crushed garnet rid it of oil. Then to make sure that they would encounter no more olive oil problems, a test laboratory was established.

Labs tests of incoming products were primitive at first. Production men were skeptical because they had learned their trade on the job by trial and error. Nine persons hired for the lab found getting along with the production crews so uncomfortable that they came and left within nine months. But 3M's research and development had gained a toehold.

From Adversity To Diversity

The olive oil story of 3M's early days working with abrasives is well-loved by this company. Experimentation led to invention of an artificial mineral and the **Three-M-ite** coated abrasive that is one of the thousands of lasting products. Ironically, adversity led to diversity. Today, 3M is known for its 60,000 products that originated more from adhesives experimentation rather than abrasives. To enable entrepreneurial activity, 3M makes $50,000 developmental grants to employees to work on ideas outside their regular assignments. They follow the rule that permits 15% of employees' time to be spent on such ideas for new products.

> *ATTITUDE & ACTION*
>
> Companies that really care about families structure work arrangements that permit flexible hours, leaves for emergencies, and sharing of jobs. Such arrangements "actually reduce absenteeism, cut turnover, save money, and boost efficiency."
>
> *--The Right Family Values in the Workplace, Business Week.*

In 1975, 3M launched a program, called "Pollution Prevention Pays," that within 20 years generated 41,000 ideas from its employees--ideas that eliminated 1.3 billion pounds of pollutants and saved the company more than $710 million. Because of employee suggestions, toilet-bowl brushes are made from left over plastic fibers used in making Scotch-Brite cleaning cloths, and the Never Rust Wool Soap Pads impregnated with nonphosphorous soap are made from recycled plastic bottles. Pollution Prevention

Pays is a family-friendly, environmentally-friendly project that also helps the bottom line.

OUR STORY SO FAR, written to celebrate their 75th anniversary, captures and highlights the values of 3M. In the accounts of the company's early days, we find the values of **enterprise, persistence, work ethic**, and **innovation** connected to family. For example, on the pages that tell the olive oil story, there is the picture of one of the founders holding his baby daughter, demonstrating that 3M values **family**. OUR STORY SO FAR includes dozens of such photos and incidents that celebrate workplace connectedness and family relationships. Consider the values that are depicted in the following happenings at various 3M locations described in that volume:

Praise & recognition
➤ Congratulations to Alan Fowler and Kathy Nesbit on their completion of 10 years of service in Sydney, Australia. There was an announcement of Lorraine Mills' birthday, although she would not reveal her age. Also, John Psaltis was named outstanding player in a match in which the 3M rugby team trounced a Maritime Services Board team 13-3.

➤ Co-workers and customers held a party to celebrate the 75th anniversary at the Tokyo American Club.

Learning & recreation
➤ Eight 3M companies of Southeast Asia met for a two-day seminar on the features, advantages and benefits of visual products and overhead transparencies.

➤ Loranzo Priorone, manager of training and education services, assembled 20 of the company's marketing personnel for an intensive week of skill-sharpening at 3M Italy.

➤ Trine Lise Nordboe, at 3M Norway near the Arctic Circle, trained a newspaper's personnel on use of a high speed copier. By late afternoon, she was able to practice handball with other 3Mers and then relax in the employees' sauna facilities. ("Yes, they are segregated, female only," she reported.)

Appreciation for talent and collective expression
➤ 3M's Male Chorus from Minnesota vacationed in Europe and presented a concert at Cergy near Paris.

Diversity
➤ Donation of all concert proceeds went to the Martin Luther King Workshop as a "good symbol" of the close relationship between the community of Minneapolis/St. Paul and 3M.

Achievement
▶ Papers were presented by Gary King, George Drossos, and Dale Tucker at 3M's London, Ontario headquarters--the best.

▶ Charles R. Whitfield, operator of a slitter machine that makes smaller and narrower consumer-size rolls out of big ones, set a plant production record with 225 cuts of filament tape during an eight-hour shift at the Bristol, Pennsylvania plant.

▶ In the city of St. Paul which houses 3M's headquarters campus, the Dispatch editor printed a birthday greeting to a "supplier of products which touch the lives of countless millions every day."

Honesty, trust, loyalty & responsibility
▶ When employees learned that corporate funds had been used to make illegal political contributions, letters with remarks such as those that follow were sent to management: "As a member of the 3M family, I was hurt deeply and felt personally betrayed." "I believe I *can* change the system by making my view known and by encouraging others, individually and corporately, to be honest and dedicated . . . And finally, I disagree that St. Paul is uninterested in my thoughts on the subject. 3M stresses and expects integrity from its employees. It follows that employees may stress and expect integrity from 3M Company."

Helpfulness, concern for others, civic pride, civility, & good citizenship

➤ During the depression when those without work stood in line for jobs that paid 25 cents an hour, 3M established its own pension fund and sickness and disability insurance. That was expanded into one of the nation's first company-paid unemployment insurance plans.

➤ The Employee Clown Club members entertained at a hospital for crippled children.

➤ 3M matches educational gifts of pensioners who retired directly from 3M on the same terms as it matches donations of current employees.

➤ A financial analyst, visiting 3M for the first time to appraise the company's performance and prospects, said he was impressed with the "free and easy" atmosphere.

➤ Purchasing agent Charles Pflager said, "The day I was hired the attitude was 180 degrees different from any other job I ever went into. In other shops, I was introduced to the foreman, and he put me to work. At 3M, I was not only introduced to my foreman, I was introduced to all the supervisors, I was introduced to the people I would be working with, I was shown how I would fit into things and right off the bat I felt part of the organization."

▶ 3M underwrites Public Broadcasting programs which address the problems of the aged, alcoholism, venereal disease, learning disabilities, and breast cancer.

> ## ATTITUDE & ACTION
>
> The lesson from such incidents as are listed from 3M's many locations is that the workplace can be the repository of the deeply held motivator of attachment and connectedness.

▶ Robert H. Tucker, when serving as the first chairman of the board of directors committee on social responsibility, said "Corporate responsibility is more than frosting on the cake. It must be part of everything we do at 3M."

▶ During a presidential election, 3M lighted its 12-story-high building so that its windows spelled out VOTE against the darkness.

▶ Harry Heltzer, board chairman in the early 1970s, when talking about the international role of business, stated, "Businesses may not always think of themselves as peacemongers. But that is what they are. And it's a title they can wear with pride."

What are the lessons we might learn from the 3M story? Myriad values are embodied in **family attitude and action:** The 3M story is one of community and connectedness. Employees' names are essential to 3M. The whole person is valued. There is appreciation of employees' health and recreation as well as their job skills and innovation. Moral integrity of the individual and how that serves as a watchdog for corporate practices is praised.

> *ATTITUDE & ACTION*
>
> "The farther society disperses physically, the more we need human connections . . . stronger and more lasting bonds of family and friendships . . . the sharing of economic troubles . . . a people who accept the stewardship of the land."
>
> *--Richard Louv in <u>America II</u>*

In <u>Our Story So Far</u>, personal advantage is not praised. Rather, we find what makes a strong corporate culture is concern for the well-being of others. The altruistic traits of helpfulness, concern for others, civic pride, and civility lubricate human interaction and make good citizens.

A company that wants its employees to put their families first demonstrates its own concern for family and family values. In turn, a family-minded workplace reaps the benefits of connectedness and is a place to which its employees are committed. Corporations that give high priority to family are particularly important at a time in our society in which the family is at risk because of teen-age unwed pregnancies, single-parent households, and in which urban anonymity has replaced community.

To Be Known By Name

In Chapter One, I made the argument that bonding is not something that is limited to mother and child. Being attached and connected is a human need that continues through life, and in the workplace. We hunger to be recognized and known by name. Sometimes that desire is manifested in unique ways--even by being difficult and different.

Air historian Robert Serling in his story of Boeing tells us of Ben Wheat, who at one time worked as a parts dispatcher and rose to vice president and general manager of Boeing's Wichita plant. Wheat was known for his sharp tongue, but was not a humorless bean counter. To make the point that the security guards were not checking identification badges, he started wearing false badges--Superman, Batman, and even Ted Bundy the convicted serial killer.

Security guards do more important work than check identification badges. When at their best, they are the greeters who with a nod will tell us if we belong as we enter the gates where we work.

Family Produces Added Value

The bottom line is so demanding that many organizations expect an employee to put job first and family second. That can cause parents to neglect their children, destroy marriages, and pit loyalty to family against commitment to the workplace.

> ### ATTITUDE & ACTION
>
> "The company with the greatest balance between work and family will win in the long run."
>
> *--Katherine Hudson, Chief Executive Officer of W.H. Brady Company headquartered in Milwaukee, Working Woman.*

Henry Ford once complained, "Why is it that I always get a whole person when what I really want is a pair of hands." Fortunately, most employers do not take such a narrow view of the value of an employee. Employers who see workers only as tenders of machines will find that they have a lot of hostile employees who can sink their companies.

Conversely, employees will want to add value to their work when they genuinely feel they are members of the corporate family--when they find that the values important to families are alive and well where they work.

Having connections is not so much knowing high-status people as it is about having a good fit between you, your family, and your work. Real connectedness entails liking of one's coworkers and respect of one's superiors; a cooperative relationship between management and union; a trusting relationship between suppliers and a firm; and a close relationship between a company and its customers and community.

COMMUNICATION AT WORK

CHAPTER THREE

HI HON, CAN YOU COME HERE?

The courts have ruled that employees can be disciplined for sexual harassment and that employers are responsible if they allow a hostile work environment. Management is liable if it engages in or does not correct a pattern of unwanted sexually suggestive messages.

These include unwanted touching, propositions, wolf whistles and nude posters. Other examples range from embarrassing sexual remarks to outright *quid pro quo* threats of no sex or no promotion or no job.

A nurse described how nervous she was when early in her career she was assigned to surgery. The surgeon was one of the big guys on the staff, she said. He and others were doing surgery on a woman; and when they got down to her pubic hair the surgeon joked about it. Continuing her story, she said, "They looked at me and made some comment about my red hair and then made a comment about whether my pubic hair matched the hair on my head. I thought I would die."

An isolated incident? Not so. A woman neurosurgeon on the staff of Stanford University School of Medicine charged that her male colleagues, throughout her career, had made jokes about her premenstrual cycle, going to bed with them, and rather than addressing her professionally would say, "Hi hon, can you come here?"

It was for a quite different work situation that the U.S. Supreme Court held that workers do not have to be emotionally damaged victims to prove that they have been harassed. Teresa Harris worked for Forklift Systems as an equipment manager for over two years. The president of Forklift, Charles Hardy, was found often to have made Ms. Harris a target of such remarks as "You're a woman, what do you know" and "We need a *man* as a rental manager." Hardy also called her a "dumb ass woman" and suggested that they "go to the Holiday Inn to negotiate [her] raise."

On one occasion, Hardy threw objects on the ground and asked the women to pick them up. When Harris complained about the offensiveness of his remarks, Hardy said he was only joking but the pattern continued. Ms. Harris sued and won. The special significance of the Forklift case is that a victim does not have to prove that sex was required to keep one's job. Nor do victims have to prove that the harassment caused them to become emotional basket cases.

Most cases are not as extreme as these examples. Those who harass are not always oafs. But crude examples are not hard to find. "Thinking about doing your man tonight? Is that why you didn't do what I told you to?" and "You don't do it that way, silly girl!" are two of many I have come across.

Too frequently those who charge sexual harassment risk their careers. My purpose in raising this topic is not to say all sexual harassment claims are valid. Nor are am I saying all sexual remarks are taboo in the workplace. One woman in a company in which I held seminars came in one day with buttons strategically pinned to her blouse and slacks with the words on each of them, "Harass me here!"

What I am saying is that a communicative attitude at work is respectful; it is professional. I am additionally stressing the high costs of a hostile work environment. Not only is it distracting and stressful for its victims, but the courts have made it expensive.

There Is No Morale Problem Here

Telxon, whose headquarters are in Akron, Ohio, makes hand-held computers. Its chief customers are companies that use its instruments to track inventory. I have followed the growth of this company because it is close to where I live. Also because I have bought its stock.

In the mid-90s, Richard Gurda, the company's vice president for corporate communications, told reporters that there was no morale problem at Telxon, rather the problem was one of communication. It was not that employees were overworked, depressed, or unappreciated. Nor was it mismanagement, although he avoided the nickname workers gave to their Chief Executive Officer Robert Meyerson--Mr. Chaos.

Nor was the problem that there were too many chiefs and not enough Indians. Telxon did not have as many vice presidents as the banks; practically

> ## ATTITUDE & ACTION
>
> Psychologist V. Jon Bentz, long-time director of Sears psychological services, has researched the reasons for poor performance of the company's high-level executives. One fatal flaw found in otherwise skilled executives was an overriding aggressive trait--a strong need to put others on the defensive and an unchecked drive for status.
>
> *--Reported by Jack Horn in <u>Psychology Today</u>*

everyone but a teller in a bank is a vp, he declared. Gurda did concede that his scheduling three separate meetings to hear employees' concerns might be interpreted as a morale problem, but he said COMMUNICATIONS would cure whatever it was.

Gurda told employees that what he called the Human Misery Department (Department of Human Resources) was done away with and its head was gone. The departure of the head of Human Misery, however, he said, was not a sign that Telxon would treat its employees as expendable. No, Telxon cares about its employees. In place of the Department of Human Misery, there now is an Employees Services Department--a place where employees can go to talk, to be heard, and get something done. Needless to say,

Telxon has a lot of work to do and I want the best for Mr. Gurda, CEO Meyerson, and the whole operation.

Communication Is More Than Information

However, I do not agree with what Mr. Gurda implies--that communications can cure whatever ails a workplace. Communication too often is thought of as

> *ATTITUDE & ACTION*
>
> Forrest Gump in Winston Groom's novel observed that most people don't look dumb till they start talkin'.

simply more information and more messages from management. But that **ain't** communication. Communication is two-way. It is sending and receiving. Speaking and listening. It is allowing for two-way influence. It is the ongoing interactive process of clarifying, verifying, and negotiating. It is a matter of making what is uncertain less uncertain. It is not telling employees what to do. It is granting them influence over their jobs and in their work organization.

An unstated purpose of organization is to deal with uncertainty. Just as we listen to weather reports to better predict what we will do tomorrow, work organizations seek data to better predict the many variables that affect doing business--such as the prime rate, the labor supply, costs and availability of raw materials, government regulation, and when they can get the best price for their products.

Those organizations which are best able to get good information can cope more effectively with the uncertainties of what some have labeled a turbulent environment.

Uncertainty reduction requires competitive intelligence. The Central Intelligence Agency's mission is to gather data important to the survival of our nation. The Federal Bureau of Investigation's mission is to gather information necessary to apprehend crime within our borders. Their purposes are to reduce the uncertainties of governing. In a similar way, competitive intelligence is needed for organizations. Sometimes companies will resort to illegal means to learn what the competition is doing. I think that is unnecessary and unethical. But I do suggest that competitive intelligence is a matter of a communicative attitude in day to day operations.

Conflict Goes With The Job

Expecting to be misunderstood can prevent some of the annoyance that comes from being misunderstood, and can prompt you to compensate for the equivocal nature of language. Misunderstandings result in mistakes, and mistakes waste rather than add value. Therefore, when we have a communicative attitude, we do not expect a message sent to someone to be acted upon perfectly; even professional quarterbacks know that their target receivers do not always catch their passes. Words are even more slippery than footballs passed in a blizzard.

Research of on-the-job conflict lends abundant evidence that misunderstandings result in serious loss. In one instance a customer complained that she did not get what she ordered. The employee responded that she served what was ordered. The customer, now becoming loud and irate, said that the employee had an attitude problem. The employee then became angry and called her manager. Later the manager advised the employee that the next time she encountered a complaining customer to call him immediately.

In another instance, a customer complained that the employee did not know how to count change. The employee told the customer to go to hell. The employee lied about his mistake, and consequently was fired. There were other cases in which employees "got smart" with customers.

Disagreements between co-workers and their superiors also result in bad morale. A younger new employee, who had graduated from a vocational school, and an older employee disagreed about their responsibilities. Each bad-mouthed the other to co-workers. The manager then set up a training seminar which was designed to improve interpersonal communication and promote a pleasant working environment. All workers had to attend. There also were numerous misunderstandings pertaining to time off, many in which both the superior and the subordinate were annoyed with each other. In some cases, employees had ideas for improvements that were rejected. One proposed redoing a shelf in a toy store to feature a new product. That suggestion was rejected outright by the manager because he said the toy was not popular. The employee, who proposed the shelving, said that he nevertheless had uncountable requests for the item because customers could not locate it. Disagreements about how jobs should be done were reported again and again.

Bosses From Hell

We have heard bosses yell and swear at their subordinates. Bosses from hell have short fuses. They are known for their explosions and verbal abuse of those around them.

Verbal abuse, not unlike physical abuse, has no place in the workplace. It creates, rather than drives out fear. A sensitive communicator is friendly, relaxed, and protective of co-workers' feelings and dignity. A communicative attitude is sensitive to others and promotes respect.

> ## *ATTITUDE & ACTION*
>
> A temporary employee in IBM's San Francisco office reported that for "Two weeks, 50 people labored 14 hours a day on an elaborate presentation with graphics and multimedia, spending thousands of dollars--all so that a few middle managers would impress" IBM's chief executive officer. Might it take a temporary employee to see the folly of such fear prompted **over-communication?**
>
> --Michael M. De Jesus
Letter to the Editor, <u>Business Week</u>.

Talking As Though Walking On Eggs

Employees sometimes become so afraid of conflict and the verbal abuse associated with it that they avoid disagreement and argument. Yet arguing can be good for the workplace. Argument deals with issues. Argument analyzes. It locates causes. It ferrets out hidden agendas, all the while being careful not to belittle another's opinion. A communicative attitude is assertive.

Vigorous argument and playing the devil's advocate help us see other positions and to consider pitfalls for a course of action. To argue with the boss, or for the boss to argue with a subordinate, conveys a measure of respect for that other person's opinion. We dismiss those opinions we do not think deserve an answer. We dare to argue only with those whom we respect enough to debate.

It takes backbone to speak up when others are more articulate. Work groups need to learn the benefits of dispute. They need to purposely play the devil's advocate. Arguing forces us to consider different points of view and to avoid the consequences of groupthink.

Modern managers know that psychological ownership of a course of action is generated by participative decision-making. But participative decision-making too often results in "committeeitis"--a disease that can be prevented by a mixture of assertiveness, respectful solicitation of other's opinions, and rigorous-vigorous analysis of what to do.

Communication Rich

In communication-deprived workplaces, the grapevine is ripe with rumors, gossip, and fear. The open door policy, widely proclaimed by most managers, is far from open. Managers themselves often are unsure of what information should be shared, and therefore, they feel safer playing their cards close to the vest.

A communication rich workplace operates under the assumption that truth is essential to trust. The more workplace information is shared on a daily basis with all employees, the more employees feel they are a part of the organization and the better they are able to judge what works and what frustrates its goals.

> *ATTITUDE & ACTION*
>
> I've never learned anything while talking. That's why we have two ears and one mouth--a place we often put our foot into.

What Do Employees Need To Know?

What information do employees need? They need to understand goals, mission, and market. This means open-book management. Most financial data should not be kept secret from workers. Of course employees' personnel data, such as their medical report, should be private. Also matters that might adversely affect a firm's competitiveness are bits of information that should be held by a select few; that is the kind of secrecy employees will respect.

Employees need to know what is at stake. They need to know how their own work connects with suppliers and with co-workers. They need to know how to do their jobs and the standards required to meet and exceed customers' expectations.

ATTITUDE & ACTION

We spin theories and rules of workplace communication, some of them true and others quite cynical:

Information travels more surely to those with a lesser need to know.
--*Charles P. Boyle, Goddard Space Flight Center, NASA.*

Information you have is not what you want.
The information you want is not what you need. The information you need is not what you can obtain.
--*Finagle's Laws of Information in Paul Dickson <u>The Official Rules</u>.*

The moment you have worked out an answer, start checking it--it probably isn't right. Most general statements are false, including this one.
--*Edmund C. Berkeley, former editor of <u>Computers and Automation</u>.*

Two-Way And Frequent

Strange as it may seem, on the wall of a conference room at the Central Intelligence Agency, probably the most secretive and quiet of all government agencies, are these rules:

1. Listen for understanding, not rebuttal.
2. Do not initiate personal attacks.

3. Recognize different communication styles and be encouraging of others.
4. Be open and honest.

Silence in organizational life is not golden. A workplace lacking frequent communication is in a state of poverty.

WORK HOARSE
vs.
CLEAR VOICE

CHAPTER FOUR

SUCCESS DEPENDS UPON UNDISTORTED INFORMATION

The success of most work organizations hinges upon how cheaply and efficiently they collect accurate information. Much of what goes on in any workplace is known best by those closest to the job. Ironically, getting undistorted information is corrupted by the employees' need to keep their bosses happy. Why that is true is more easily explained than is remedied. Subordinates' pay and job security are tied to their superiors' evaluation of them. Consequently, they naturally want to say what bosses want to hear and they tend to be silent about what they think will reflect badly upon them.

Bootlicking Hurts Employee Voice

Some few bosses are open to bad news and even can be trusted not to retaliate if those lower in the chain of command argue with them. Other bossy bosses enjoy being surrounded by bootlicking subordinates. Managers, of course, also have bosses and also know that breaking the "keep the boss happy" rule has unwanted consequences. Therefore, managers tend to give less and less weight to opinions of subordinates and it follows that their decision making become more and more centralized.

There is no easy fix to get workers to speak the truth. Yet continuous quality improvement and high performance depend upon on workers' willingness to say what is wrong and to risk expressing their ideas. As managers increasingly realize that, they encourage employee voice.

Workers' Range Of Voice

Voice comes in different forms. Employees who see things that they would like changed in their work environment have four alternatives:

- to keep their mouths shut and remain loyal workers
- to neglect their jobs, reduce their efforts, murmur dissatisfaction, be late or absent, be careless with equipment, sabotage and steal from their companies
- to exit, and possibly by leaving to stimulate their employers to change that which caused the dissatisfaction
- to speak up, to make constructive suggestions, to take one's complaints through grievance channels, and if wrongdoing is illegal, reporting that to those in charge, and if that is unsuccessful, blowing the whistle by going to the press or to the law.

Each working day employees have a range of voice behaviors that follow these four alternatives. Short of voting with one's feet, by voluntary exit from the organization, active voice is the only viable way to stimulate change. How that desired change is phrased in active voice is a matter of persuasion.

Voice is more likely to influence change when it has earned credibility. Workers earn credibility by a history of dependability and supportiveness. Both good sense and good character come into play when we want to influence change. Small changes can be stimulated by well-timed questions. Larger changes need to be presented in cost-benefit proposals. Once continuous quality improvement has been adopted as the way a workplace operates, worker voice is welcomed and encouraged.

Anti-Union, Anti-Voice

Unions are a form of organized employee voice, organizations that have a history of struggle and bloodshed. During the late 1800s and the first third of the 1900s, labor was intimidated by employer-hired thugs and battered in its attempts to organize. Sometimes workers themselves bullied their coworkers and employers. Unfortunately, some union leaders have been greedy, corrupt and a few self-serving managers have engaged in bullying anti-union campaigns. The 1935 National Labor Relations Act guaranteed labor the right to organize and to bargain. Following that legislation, unions grew strong.

That is not the case for unions today. Their power and punch is lightweight. Membership has declined until only approximately 11% of private industry is unionized and may decline farther to single digits. Total union membership is about 16 million or 15% of the workforce.

Following declining membership, workers have suffered a turn south in wages, health benefits, and pension plans. Moreover, without unions, employers are freer to fire workers for any reason as they will. Consequently, there has been an increase in unlawful-discharge suits.

Old-time labor-management battles are not only past history. Protracted bitter lose-lose wars continue in this decade, such as between Caterpillar's management and the United Auto Workers and baseball owners and the players' union. Because of labor-management's history of adversarial strife, managers will not readily swallow any proposal for union-management partnership. We know that. But we also know until mutual respect for each other's expertise replaces labor-management badmouthing each other, quality improvement efforts will be frustrated.

Business Week reporter Aaron Bernstein, in a lengthy look at the advantages and disadvantages of unions, acknowledged that most employers would be delighted if unions would disappear. Over the past dozen years, he states "U.S. industry has conducted one of the most successful anti-union wars ever, illegally firing thousands of workers for exercising their right to organize." Yet he argues that a new

unionism can advance corporate competitiveness rather than frustrate it as old adversarial unionism too often did.
And he singles out such captains of industry who have been able to work collaboratively with unions. Among these are LTV's Chief Executive David H. Hoage, Ford's head of cooperative labor programs Ernest J. Savoie, and Xerox's CEO Paul A. Allaire, who says just that: "I don't want to say we need unions if that means the old, adversarial kind. But if we had a cooperative model, the union movement will be sustained and the industries it's in will be more competitive."

The Voice Of Partnership

Xerox's partnership with the Amalgamated Clothing & Textile Workers Union (ACTWU) is the kind of new unionism that Allaire has in mind: one that encourages flexibility and a team effort; one in which management shares internal financial documents with union officials and provides them the same kind of training in accounting and financial matters that its managers take.
In the mid 90s, the AFL-CIO Committee on the Evolution of Work issued its report, <u>The New American Workplace: A Labor Perspective</u>. This report charts a course for union action that most employers should find supportive of their strategy to become world class. The overarching theme of this

report calls for forming partnerships between unions and management. Forming partnerships entail:

➤ a redistribution of decision-making authority from management to workers who are often organized in teams. This means workers are helped to develop skills necessary to many of the decisions previously restricted to management. The report rejects the division between mental and manual labor in which workers are asked to "check their brains at the door."

➤ that no longer should there be rigid job definitions; jobs should call for a greater variety of skills and degree of responsibility. Workers should understand the complete production or service process.

➤ flatter management structure; managers serve as leaders and facilitators rather than bosses.

➤ workers, through their unions, are enjoined in decision-making roles at all levels of an enterprise.

➤ rewards from reorganization of work are distributed equitably between labor and management through negotiation.

The New American Workplace: A Labor Perspective does much to put to bed the past adversarial stance of unions. A dialogue is beginning. Transformation takes time.

Unlike most other authors on quality and customer awareness, I argue that worker voice should be encouraged both within the workgroup in team-constructive ways and within worker unions. Democracy entails mechanisms for negotiation, due process for wrongful discharge, and for balancing the power of employers and management. To the extent that employees become significant shareholders in a democratically managed workplace, unions may be less necessary, but nevertheless are important mechanisms for representing the interest of labor regionally, nationally, and internationally, just as are national and international manufacturing, business and professional associations.

Critical Involvement

Whether or not an organization has a union, encouraging workers to voice their concerns has practical benefits. Those benefits include:
- employee involvement and commitment to meeting customer requirements
- generating a desire to follow instructions
- nurturing morale
- preventing frustrated workers from badmouthing the workplace and from thinking that the only way to deal with what employees think is wrong is to blow the whistle.

There is value added from critical involvement of employees. There is special value when employees care enough to voice their concerns about something that is terribly wrong.

> ## ATTITUDE & ACTION
>
> Motivations for encouraging workers to voice their concerns are practical, psychic, and moral. **Practical** because unless workers want to talk about ways to do their jobs better little quality improvement is possible. **Psychic** because our voices are the way we express our frustration and aspiration. To squelch workers voice is to alienate and dampen psychological well-being. **Moral** because humans have ideals and those ideals are most constructively expressed through democratic channels.

Consider the major fiascos that might have been prevented if managers, engineers, and workers had had been encouraged to make their voices heard: the coverup by Johns Manville of the dangers of asbestos; the disastrous consequences of the Dalkon Shield interuterine device and of silicone breast implants; the near meltdown at Three Mile Island; the mishandling of nuclear production at Rocky Flats and Hansford; the cost overruns in the Department of Defense such as the alleged $20 billion overcharge in building the Stealth bomber; the abortive Bay of Pigs invasion, the Challenger disaster that engineers had predicted and the multimillion dollar error of the distorted Hubble telescope; and the Savings and Loan scandal.

Whether organized or not, employees have a range of voice. Employers should realize that value-added attitude and action simply do not happen when worker voice is squelched or stilled out of fear. A communicative attitude and action is the *sin qua non*, the without which any quality effort can prosper.

Voiceless

Our sanity is maintained by tuning out much of the noise we hear. Our humanity, however, is determined by how well we listen. We can not help but attend to those with powerful voices. They are the shapers of the workplace and society. But really listening is to hear those with weak voices and to know that what is not said may speak even more loudly. Weak voices have little or no say; they are the disempowered.

Who are the voiceless? They are those who are not mentioned when decisions are made. They are the temporaries, the part-time employed, the low-skilled, and those who work at minimum wage. In many workplaces, minorities and women have little say. Outside the workplace in every community, the voiceless are the jobless and those in poverty. The voiceless include the children, the physically and mentally disadvantaged, those on the fringes and in prison, and those yet to be born who will have to live in the environment we leave them. Those who have little of no voice are the neglected, the negated, and the oppressed.

Enabling those with little voice to speak is the goal of education, job training, and equal opportunity legislation. Making voices stronger requires increasing both individual competencies and self-esteem. We should not fear empowering the voiceless for equality of voice is the fundamental tenet of democracy. Giving "we the people" voice is the strength of America. It is a paradox that hearing what is not said can add value to the workplace and most certainly enriches our humanity.

WE WILL NOT GIVE QUALITY...

CHAPTER FIVE

What The Customer Wants

Attentiveness to customer wants requires an ear to the ground. Product quality is not simply delivering what the manufacturer determines will please the customer. Talk about excellence is meaningless unless it is spelled out in the user's language and definition.

Rather than general talk about excellence, quality does not happen unless it is carefully defined in terms of what the customer says is needed. Customers define requirements in. . .

- technological terms such as hardness, functional use, and measurement specifications.
- time-oriented terms such as consistency reliability, maintainability, durability, repair costs, and promptness of delivery.
- contractual terms such as guarantee provisions.
- psychological terms such as taste, beauty, and status.
- ethical terms such as courtesy and honesty of the personnel.

Three God-Words

Management continuously searches for symbols, slogans, and programs that will motivate. During this past decade three words have taken on sacred proportion: **Total Quality Management,** in shorthand TQM. Total Quality Management has become so popular that everyone wants to claim it.

Unfortunately in many companies, TQM is more rhetoric than substance. TQM departments, which have grown exponentially, too often have boasted quality improvements that are not backed up by return on investment. Consequently, the consultants are ready and eager to provide new lingo, such as Return on Quality.

> *ATTITUDE & ACTION*
>
> Perhaps the most important motto any organization can have is simply:
>
> WE WILL NOT GIVE
> QUALITY A BAD NAME!

Top management, because it must be concerned about the bottom line, wants language that emphasizes profits, hence the new label Return On Quality (ROQ). Consultant John Murphy, president of Executive Edge, claims to have originated and to own the trademark registration for ROQ.

Cut The Slogans

A similar problem to the tarnish of TQM has occurred with the International Standards ISO 9000 series, which emphasizes certification programs for

European products. Requiring certification is far easier than infusing quality into the workplace.

The guru of quality, W. Edwards Deming, was so distressed by how quickly slogans touting quality became sullied that he preached that slogans should be avoided. He rather emphasized that management decisions should be based upon hard data.

Let me add that over-attention to hard data is a mistake. Some things can and should be measured, but too much charting wastes time. In one plant in which I trained, machine operators were required to record stacks of computer data that were never looked at.

Trying to get a baseline for every practice is futile and does not meet the cost-effective goal of Return On Quality. Quarterly financial reports on all quality improvements in my opinion are misplaced. Such efforts waste valuable time and generate fear and sometimes even distort the numbers.

The Quality Movement

The quality movement began after World War II when Japan was hurting. W. Edwards Deming and Joseph Juran, both early U.S. proponents of translating management into measurement systems, carried that message to Japan which was devastated by war and had a reputation for cheap exports. These men found a receptive management and a work culture that believed in details and training.

The statistical tools the Japanese borrowed from the U.S. fit well into that country. The Japanese honor training, knowledge, authority, and group processes. Training in statistics enabled standardization and therefore provided exacting tools for reducing variation and for experimenting with ways to reduce cycle time. Training took the tools of engineers to the shop floor, thus empowering workers. Within two decades, major Japanese industries were taking market share from U.S. producers of electronics and automobiles.

Kaizen, the notion of continuous incremental improvement in quality, had found fertile soil. *Ringi*, the notion of group problem-solving and circulating proposals for consensus, also was compatible with the Japanese values of harmony and homogeneity. Add to this, the respect for authority and a high work ethic and you have a nation that rose like the phoenix.

The moral reason for striving to make quality products and to deliver quality service is our motivation to do good and not do harm. But are there also practical reasons for delivering the best possible? The answer is a resounding **YES**. Quality in practical terms means making a product that is stronger than required, is free from harm to people and the environment, and is easily repaired. Companies that deliver robust quality have lower overall costs because they will have fewer recalls, fewer legal penalties, and quicker repairs.

The Ongoing Improvement Process

The U.S. largely has results-focused management whereas Japan has kaizen process-oriented management. For the Japanese, kaizen is the ongoing improvement process in the lives of all individuals. That is something that U.S. quality managers seem to miss.

> ### ATTITUDE & ACTION
>
> Getting to quality and high performance misses the mark if it is conceived of as profits and beating the competition. Innovation and improvement will more naturally happen if nurtured as individual skill and character development.

Managers know that business is meeting the numbers. Their task is to increase efficiency, market share, stock prices, and profits. In addition to business savvy, accomplishing those goals requires corporate cheerleading. Rhetoric, however, will sound hollow and quality programs will turn sour unless they are linked to the motives of the heart--as spelled out in corporate commitment to its workforce, spelled out in corporate attention to community well-being, and spelled out in individual and corporate integrity.

Following the Japanese, we formed quality circles (QC) and taught statistical process control (SPC). The gurus of quality in a foreign land were now welcomed home. Evangelists such as Tom Peters and Robert Waterman captured the imagination of management in their book <u>In Search of Excellence</u>. The American Society for Quality Control took on national status and developed certification for quality specialists and engineers.

Building upon the American penchant for competition and winning, the National Institute of Standards and Technology established the Malcolm Baldrige National Quality Awards, to match Japan's W. Edwards Deming Prize.

Hewlett-Packard was spurred on by the quick turnaround of a Japanese joint venture. Building upon the quality principles of Genichi Taguchi, in five short years, Yokogawa HP of Japan won the Deming prize.

John Young, HP's Chief Executive Officer, called for a ten-fold improvement in hardware reliability during the 1980s. Even before the end of that decade, HP could boast $400 million in savings of warranty costs due to renewed emphasis on hardware quality.

Data from companies such as HP bolstered the razzle-dazzle of continuous quality improvement programs. Programs such as Organizational Development were abandoned for the immaculate new idea of Total Quality Management. Baldrige winners were reported ahead of the pack. Their stock prices rose, with a few exceptions such as IBM's unexpected decline and Wallace Company's near bankruptcy. A General Accounting Office survey of the top 20 in competition for the Baldrige award indicated that these companies had improvements in market share, sales per employee, return on assets, and on-time delivery of their products.

TQM As Service

Worship of quality improvement too frequently is treated as cutting waste and zero defects--and as a tool kit for efficiency. Those tools, top managers say they most often use, are in descending popularity: mission statements, customer surveys, Total Quality Management, benchmarking, and reengineering.

A recent study of 463 companies, however, found no correlation between a tool's popularity and the user's financial performance. Rather, mission statements, the most widely used, correlated with below-average financial results. Customer surveys, the second most used tool, appeared to provide the most benefit.

The quality movement is rooted in manufacturing. Statistical process control, reduction in cycle time, benchmarking, redesign of products, reengineering, and Total Quality Management, all center upon production. Much of the emphasis in manufacturing has been upon tooling and calibration, and upon taking the people variable skills out of the quality equation.

Total Quality Management too often is a management-initiated program designed to speed up production. Also TQM sometimes has faltered because a bureaucracy of quality control personnel evolves parallel to the managerial chain of command. That makes for more rather than less production costs and creates destructive conflict.

> ## *ATTITUDE & ACTION*
>
> "A learning business today is one that leverages the economic value of knowledge. **It is always figuring out how to define, acquire, develop, apply, measure, grow, use, multiply, protect, transfer, sell, profit by, and celebrate the company's know-how.**"
>
> --Stan Davis and Jim Botkin in *The Monster Under The Bed: How Business Is Mastering the Opportunity of Knowledge for Profit*

Despite these limitations, Total Quality Management has raised the consciousness that within a plant each operation is a customer of another operation. TQM's attention to the internal customer has brought a new awareness to the interdependence of all who are there to serve the end customers. TQM additionally has enhanced our awareness that the ultimate test is the external customer's satisfaction and confidence. Even for manufacturing, the ultimate test is delivery and service of a product. Buying a Lexus has come to mean luxury service, not just purchase of a luxury car.

Today 4 out of 5 workers are in the service sector. Ronald Henkoff in <u>Fortune</u> says that "These legions of customer-contact workers make up one of the fastest-growing--and least appreciated--segments of the U.S. labor force." To be sure, measuring service quality is less exacting than accounting statistically for variations in product specifications. Service quality is more interpersonal, more people to people, more relational. So it is that the quality of service delivered can differentiate one company from another.

Benchmarking & Going For The Gold

One of the strengths of the quality movement is its willingness to share what is learned with other companies. Baldrige winners must disseminate what they have learned about quality improvement. **Benchmarking**, therefore, has become standard practice.

Two years after being named Chief Executive Officer of General Motors, Jack Smith told GM shareholders, "Our corporate vision is to be the world leader in transportation products and services." But he added that "It is difficult to push the message all the way down in the organization, and I can't tell you we're there yet." Probably the most tangible way GM is making its vision real is to **benchmark** its operations against the best in class. Therefore at GM, there is a lot of talk about Toyota.

A group of ten people is charged with coordinating GM's benchmarking activities. An indicator of willingness to learn from the best is also seen in Xerox's company magazine named the Benchmark.

> *ATTITUDE & ACTION*
>
> The quality of service delivered can differentiate one company from another.

Today's standards are global world class. If the American workplace is to give a world class performance, it must take a lesson from how we train our Olympic athletes. It is a long process that begins with healthy, disciplined, motivated young people. It is a scientific process that entails skilled coaching and systematic training. Going for the gold takes a national commitment, and continuously perfecting what is already very good.

CLOSE TO THE CUSTOMER

CHAPTER SIX

Everyone Is A Customer

All of us are consumers. We each have horror stories about being treated badly by I-don't-give-a-damn clerks. Too often, we come away saying, "That person didn't really want to sell me anything. He didn't want to be bothered." I called a large department store to ask if it carried Florsheim shoes. The individual who answered the phone said, "You've got the catalog department." I was told, "I don't know

> *ATTITUDE & ACTION*
>
> What bothers you most about renewing your driver's license: Waiting in line? The eye exam? Getting a bad picture? Wouldn't we all feel better about the Department of Motor Vehicles if those who make the photo we will carry on our license took a little more care about getting a good picture?

if we carry that brand of shoe." Then when I asked to be transferred to the shoe department, the answer I got was "You'll have to look up the number." When I reported this I-just-work-here employee to the manager of human resources, a friend of mine, she was aghast.

A Leaky Bureaucracy

Despite the fact that most public employees work very hard, the workplace bureaucracy too often frustrates those it is supposed to serve. Sometimes the mistakes are terribly costly. In 1992, Chicago had a breakdown in services. It was not because of indifferent employees, but because of decision delays in the system. It was a leak that if handled immediately could have been corrected with $10,000, but rather cost an estimated $1.7 billion. On January 14, two cable TV workers came upon a 20-foot crack in a tunnel. They videotaped this, but did not know which government agency should be told of the problem.

In late February, they finally informed the proper city official and urged that the tunnel be inspected. On March 2, they learned that nothing had yet been done. Photographs were taken but a week went by waiting for their development. On April 2, a city engineer sent a memo urging immediate action. Two bids were obtained, but those were turned down in hopes of obtaining a lower bid.

On April 13, three months after the crack was first discovered, the river broke through. City hall, office towers, and the Chicago Board of trade all were shut down. Heads rolled. Those blamed were fired. The problem, however, was not the bad intentions of those responsible. The problem was a system not prepared to do preventive work or to act quickly in case of an emergency. The notion that business and the general public were the city's customers seemed so remote that delay upon delay brought on a costly flood.

Perhaps value-added attitude and action are even more needed in the public sector than in the private. I, like you, have seen road crews that appear to do more standing around than work. We have seen the police come down with the "blue flu." We have seen our

> ## ATTITUDE & ACTION
>
> "They aren't customers. They are just the people I work with." "She's not a customer. She's just my boss." "I'm not a customer. I just work here." Three statements that are dead wrong. Co-workers are each other's customers. Thinking of each other in that light makes a difference.

share of graft. We have been frustrated by the overkill of government regulations and we've seen red tape delay the clean up of toxic waste. We also know the lack of urgency that too often is endemic with public agencies that can demoralize high-energy public employees.

Government has been designed to rule out the profit motive and individual monetary gain. Despite that restriction, I have seen value-added spirit come alive in community leadership and service enhancement programs. Governing democratically is not easy. Making it work hinges upon a can-do attitude and action.

Suppliers and Customers

There are few if any workplaces that are not themselves both suppliers and customers. One poultry firm I know well has its own hatchery and contracts thousands of laying hens. Millions of chicks hatch each day to be grown on farms in the surrounding countryside. This firm has its own mills which supply feed to the growers. On the processing end, truckloads of crated live poultry are brought to its processing facilities for slaughter. This company even has purchased an ice company to ice down its fresh meats and a fleet of refrigerated trucks to take its finished meat to market.

From egg to market, it seems like an independent business. Not so. This company is a customer in hundreds of ways, such as buying feed for its mills, purchasing antibiotics to prevent disease in its flocks, ordering packaging for its finished products, hiring catering in its workers' cafeteria, negotiating loans from banks to finance building new facilities, etc.

None of us is independent. The best we can do is dream that we have so much money coming in that it doesn't matter if we mismanage it.

Most companies do their best to be wise consumers. They buy in large quantities. Like managers of commercial buildings, sometimes they form associations to bargain and buy cooperatively. We insist that our government agencies get blind bids for special purchases. Traditionally, companies force a number of vendors to compete on price and service. They are hard-nosed and do not want to be overly dependent on one supplier. They prefer to have several vendors in the wings should one of them break a leg and have difficulty in meeting their orders.

> *ATTITUDE & ACTION*
>
> "Niceness is a competitive weapon."
>
> *--A motto in an executive's office of America Online, the fastest-growing seller of on-line computer services.*

Big companies can call the shots. Motorola, as part of its great quality thrust to cut defects to two or three units per million, dropped hundreds of suppliers who would not follow the same kind of quality improvement efforts that it was undertaking. In similar fashion, General Motors demanded of its smaller suppliers a rigorous self-study and evaluation report that required hundreds of hours. Yet even after receiving an excellent report rating, these suppliers could not count on future orders. They could be under-priced and dropped.

Hard-knuckle purchasing practices do produce price cuts by suppliers. General Motors knows that has paid off. But treating suppliers as expendable makes it difficult for them to plan ahead for capacity, equipment and people. Vendors complain the drawings that their own engineers propose to GM are sometimes disclosed to other vendors to learn if they can make the parts cheaper. That practice makes them angry, secretive and grudgingly cooperative while selling to rivals of GM. One was quoted as saying, "We're not gonna bust our fanny for [GM] anymore."

Supplier relationships need not be antagonistic or fawning, but they will be unless suppliers are treated like the essential partners they should be. Such is the relationship between the GM-Toyota NUMMI operation in Fremont, California and its 300 suppliers. I believe that U.S. automakers increasingly will see the cost advantages of working closely with suppliers-- of treating them as valued partners rather than as expendable and groveling. Long-term commitment between companies with important suppliers can be made more solid with joint cost reduction efforts and profit-sharing.

Most Favored Customer Status

Coke and McDonald's have had a long-lasting love affair. McDonald's CEO Mike Quinlan glows when he talks of Coca-Cola, "They are our partner." Don Keough, Coke's former second in command and now a McDonald's board member, says, "It's an enormously important strategic alliance. McDonald's is a hallmark customer." The Coca-Cola McDonald's partnership is so firm that for a McDonald's restaurant to serve a Pepsi would be an unforgivable sin!

The traditional at-arms-length supplier-customer relationship of the past is fraught with anxiety and animosity. We, as individuals and as organizations, want to be treated as most favored customers. How can that happen?

Gathering customer feedback is one way to learn how **satisfied** customers are with products and service. Such measures are common. When well designed, they are helpful indicators of immediate product and service problems. What they do not tell is the **confidence** that a customer has in a supplier. For a supplier to earn a customer's confidence, it needs to develop a good working relationship. And that requires frequent communication about what is needed, what is delivered, and what needs to be improved.

UPS recently learned that on-time delivery was not as important as it had thought. Customers rather wanted more interaction with drivers enabling them to get advice on shipping. Consequently, UPS has relaxed its time and motion studies and pressure upon drivers to keep moving. Instead it encourages them to be a bit less hurried. Time is built into schedules for them to get out of their trucks and to chat for a few moments with customers.

Working with suppliers to achieve a high level of confidence is not something that can be achieved by the purchasing department alone. Rather those who actually use the products daily--the machine operators, the engineers, the maintenance crews--are the ones who can by face-to-face and phone-to-phone establish and nurture that supplier-customer relationship. **Learning from one's suppliers entails frequent communication--listening to them, soliciting their ideas, treating them as partners, and bringing their voices in-house.** And this same principle applies to customers.

What customers really want is not simply to be satisfied with a product or service, what they really want is **confidence** in a supplier. Once confidence is established, companies can cut the costs of inspection of incoming supplies. A supplier-customer partnership saves time, money, and headaches. It is frontline customer-contacts who best can learn what customers say they need. Let us repeat for emphasis: **Learning from customers entails frequent communication with them--listening to them, soliciting their feedback, bringing their voices in-house.**

Getting close to the customer also means thinking about needs that are not articulated. Customers don't always know what is best, because what is best is yet to be invented. Chrysler said that it did not get one request asking it to invent the minivan. Companies which think ahead about unvoiced needs are shaping customer wants. Government agencies that learn about diseases that can become epidemics help shape citizen behavior by information campaigns.

Volunteer agencies, such as the Gray Panthers, because they know their constituency's difficult present and future circumstances, can give voice to those who are feeble and have little voice. Getting close to customers, thus, means more than simply satisfying conscious needs; it means thinking for them about their future.

TOGETHER
EVERYONE
ACHIEVES
MORE

CHAPTER SEVEN

TEAMS ARE PARTNERSHIPS

Boeing's innovative computer design process for its new giant aircraft is not without customer input. From the beginning, those slated to use Boeing's new planes are invited to confer with the designers. Buyers are even invited to sit in a mockup of a new plane's interior.

Customer confidence hinges upon customer support. At one point Boeing took the heat from European customers for lack of support. A meeting was called of 40 airlines, all Boeing customers. Boeing was told its support was terrible! Some airlines had not seen people from Seattle for several years. That changed. A sign of that change is the story of a British Airways 747 that flew through a cloud of volcanic ash over Indonesia. All four engines flamed out and the plane fell from 37,000 to 12,000 feet before the crew got the engines restarted. The captain radioed "Mayday," and was able to emergency land the plane 44 minutes later in Jakarta. The first person to meet the plane was a Boeing man.

Another story told of Boeing's attention to customers is that of American Airlines CEO Bob Crandall's complaint about a reading light that went out on a passenger. Boeing first tried to explain the difficulty in wiring lights with bulbs that could easily be changed should they burn out. So that they did not have to make such excuses, the engineers went to

Value Added Attitude And Action

work. On their next airplane, the 777, a bulb could be changed by a flight attendant.

Increasingly, teams are the way work is best performed. One of the keys to the phenomenal success of 15,000 McDonald's stores comes from the first rule found in its <u>Lost Art School of Management</u>: "Gather your people often for face-to-face meetings to learn from each other."

Perhaps it's because modern organizations are so huge and individual identity gets lost that teams have become so important. Teams, rather than making the individual less important, make each person more essential.

The team-organized workplace, thus, is a place in which less is more. Tom Peters, in <u>Liberation Management</u>, after describing how today's traditional military and pyramidal structures **stink**, asserts that "You can organize a giant firm as a collection of 10-person, highly accountable teams--ever shifting and seldom at home. Moreover, word of mouth still can--and does--work as the chief 'organizing' device."

General Manager of Olin Pool Products Doug Cahill upset his 14 department structure by changing it into eight process teams. He christened the teams with names such as **resources, new products,** and **fulfillment** and ringed the eight teams about a central core labeled **customer**. Doug says he wants "an organization so flat that you could stick it under a door."

Many Different Varieties

Teams come in five variations: management teams, quality circles, natural work groups, ad hoc problem-solving teams, and dispersed teams. Management teams are composed of heads of departments. They usually meet weekly or monthly to help integrate on-going operations and to prevent or resolve conflict of interest among their units.

Quality circles in this country are composed of lower level employees who volunteer to meet to work on cost-cutting and improvement of work processes. In Japan, where QCs were instrumental in Japanese industry's surge to high quality products, they were not voluntary.

In this country, QCs are being replaced by ad hoc problem-solving teams that work on specific production and delivery problems and projects. Once these problems are solved or projects are completed, ad hoc teams are disbanded. In massive projects such as designing and building Boeing's 777, project teams functioned at many levels. Those projects involved 500 suppliers and 10,000 employees. There were design teams that worked with customers. Tail, wing, and flap teams.

Management and integrative teams helped resolve conflicts. Since coordination is often a major problem among widely dispersed plants, dispersed teams communicate by conference calls, fax, and computer.

In Different Configurations

In geometry class, we were told that a line was the shortest distance between two points. Following that principle in 1908, Henry Ford revolutionized manufacturing by adopting interchangeable parts for his cars and introducing the conveyor line. Craftsmanship is not necessary for workers who must do simple repetitive tasks, and most industries copied Ford's shortest-distance-between-two-points principle.

Today that principle has been shown not to be the most efficient for some industries. In place of the conveyor belt, we find various configurations: In a small snail-shaped shop, four workers clustered about a table completely assemble camcorders for Sony, and more such work groups in spiral arrangement have replaced the previous assembly line of 50 workers. Assembly cells are employed by Compaq Computer in Scotland and Texas in which one person fetches parts, another builds components, and two individuals assemble whole units. Other plants are tailoring minishop operations to their unique production needs in oddly shaped lines--in Ys, 6s, and three-legged spider configurations.

Small team assembly is freed from conveyor-pacing. If something goes wrong, a long line of workers does not come to a halt. Gains of 35 to 50 percent in productivity have resulted from such changes. Craftsmanship, thus, is returning to manufacturing. Extensive cross-training and apprenticeship are essential to such a change. And those in these teams gain a sense of pride in the wholeness of their work.

The natural self-managing work group, such as the assembly teams that Volvo employs in some of its plants, is one of the most practical kinds of teams. The Volvo team-assembly line has enabled job rotation, skill enrichment, and a respite from mind-numbing repetition. It is an experiment in job-design that is undergoing modification. Volvo closed some of its much publicized team-assembly lines in two of its plants. As technology changes, job configurations also change.

Craft-based layouts, of course, are not applicable to all kinds of products. Different work configurations are needed for around-the-clock continuous-flow operations of chemical plants, gasoline distilleries, and paper manufacturing.

Not All Harmony And Song

A word of caution is in order because teamwork is not all harmony and song. People who work together will have differences of opinion about how jobs should be done. They also will differ in personality and in manners. Therefore, learning to work cooperatively with civility is essential to the team-building agenda.

Those who would begin a company-wide team approach to continuous quality improvement should involve the work force in careful planning. Teamwork will become a dirty word lacking psychological ownership, management commitment, and group communication training. Converting to a team-based organization sometimes entails reassignment of some personnel and coaching teams to work with other teams. Also some jobs will be more effectively accomplished by individuals who work best alone.

Workers naturally are anxious about how teams will work. Julia Garcia, who has worked for PepsiCo Inc. Frito-Lay unit in Lubbock, Texas expressed her uneasiness, "It kind of frightened me at first. I thought, 'I'm not going to be able to decide anything.'" But after three years working within a team, her anxiety was gone, and she said "I really enjoy [the team approach] because it gives me a sense of pride." Despite less supervision due to teams, that plant has made sizeable cost cuts and has seen its quality soar to be near the top of Frito's 48 plants.

Team Problem Solving

At Ford, Quality is No. 1 is spelled out in many ways such as in its 8D Problem-Solving Process. Notice that the eight steps in that process begin and end with team:

D1. Use a team approach.
D2. Describe and verify the problem.
D3. Implement and verify interim (containment) actions.

D4. Define and verify root causes.
D5. Verify corrective actions.
D6. Choose and implement permanent corrective actions.
D7. Prevent recurrence.
D8. Congratulate the team.

> *ATTITUDE & ACTION*
>
> "Japan and Germany, the countries that are outperforming America in international trade, do not have less government or more motivated individuals. They are countries noted for their careful organization of teams--teams that involve workers and managers, teams that involve suppliers and customers, teams that involve government and business."
>
> --Lester Thurow in <u>Head to Head.</u>

Alex Trotman, chairman and chief executive officer of Ford, says that "Teamwork, like commitment, is also fundamental if you want to be the best." And he likens the 8D process to peeling off layers of an onion to find what is really inside. For example in analyzing a fuel-injection problem, teams assigned to the problem discovered that fuel tanks were not being cleaned as scrupulously as they were supposed to be during the manufacturing. Therefore, tiny metal fragments in the fuel tank would find their way into the fuel injectors. The 8D Problem-Solving Process discovered that the fuel-injection problem was really a fuel-tank problem.

Ford is creating a computer data base of such 8D problem-solving. A team will be able to quickly learn if the problem it is facing or one like it has a history, and if so, how such problems have been resolved in the past, perhaps in some other Ford plant.

Trotman, when speaking about the partnership Ford has with the UAW, quotes the United Auto Workers vice president, Ernie Lofton saying, "We're in this boat together. It's not *management and us* or *white collars and the blue collars*. We're all in the same boat and if the boat sinks, we're all going down with it."

The Rules Of Teamwork

Teamwork requires special attention to communication. Teams work best where **praise** comes easily. We see praise bubble up when teams compete. Sometimes its a high five between a quarterback and receiver after completing a pass. It may be a word of encouragement after missing a lay-up or foul shot. After a touchdown, there is the giddy dance of accomplishment, the wild pile-on hugfest, and the roar of those of us in the bleachers. And there is the ritual of cutting down the net after winning a basketball tournament.

The workplace, like the sports arena, goes better when teams acknowledge each other's accomplishments. To praise, as Aristotle said many centuries ago, is akin to urging a course of action. Praise is best which is honest, specific, and enthusiastic. Praise generates respect and is not easily overdone. Those who first acknowledge each other's good work are better received when they later question or criticize.

A second rule for team communication is **to talk over how well things are going**. Work groups need to set aside some time each day or week to review how well the team is working as a team. Making talk-over time a habit okays talk about problems and provides a time for coming to agreement upon changes.

A third rule and corrolary to talk-over time is **keep each other informed on a daily basis**. No rule is more important than this keep-me-informed rule. Workers' most frequent complaints are "nobody told me" and "management doesn't communicate." All members of a team need and want to know the plays being called!

A fourth rule for team communication is **share blame and share credit**. Rather than "I did it," try the following: "*We* did it." "*We* will correct it." "*We* are happy about it." Talk-over time can be used to discover the whys about something that went wrong and ways to prevent it in the future. Team members should be specific about how much advice they want. It is better to ask, "Am I giving you the quality material you need?" than to ask generally, "How am I doing?"

A fifth rule is **be candid but tentative**. When team members really think something is wrong, they should say so. If that something wrong is something that is dangerous, or if silence can allow for much wasted effort or cause costly rework, they should speak up immediately. However, if that something wrong is not a crisis situation, it is a topic that can be set aside for a team talk-over session. At such times, criticism will be better received if prefaced with "I thought most of what we've been doing is good, but something that has been bothering me is ..."

ATTITUDE & ACTION

"If you really believe that something is the right thing to do, don't waste too much time trying to prove it--just do it. It might cost you money, but I have no doubt that excellent quality will pay off in the long term."
   --Alex Trotman, chairman of Ford Motor Company and of National Quality Month.

A sixth rule is **allow for team member autonomy and responsibility**. Teamwork goes best when individuals bring special expertise to the team.

Some of us are more skilled and prefer some tasks over others. Making certain workers responsible for specific assignments saves time, avoids unwanted conflict, and conveys space for self-achievement. Not everyone needs to be in on every detail of every job. Allowing for team member autonomy, however, does not mean that only certain persons are forever assigned to one task. Cross-training and job rotation within the team have many benefits, such as prevention of carpal tunnel syndrome, boredom, and being able to do the job when someone is absent.

A seventh rule for team communication is **make argument acceptable**. Continuous quality improvement is frustrated by team conformity. Getting along should not dampen vigorous dispute about better ways of doing an operation. Mavericks should not be cut off from expressing opinions. When there is debate without a compelling argument, side with the ones who feel more passionately about a matter.

An eighth rule is the **explore it, trial run** principle. Team decision-making should be approached as scientists do. Before deciding on a solution, researchers investigate the nature of a problem and its various causes. They generate a range of possible solutions. Then they do trial runs to test those most likely solutions. Teams need to learn how to brainstorm. They need to learn how to systematically analyze and problem-solve. Finally, to make good decisions, teams need to learn how to collect data and to do accurate measurement before, during and after trials.

A ninth rule for effective team communication is **shared leadership**. Teams learn how to take advice from organizational coaches. They also discover that more than one member within their group has leadership abilities. Teams find that they can rotate leadership roles and that some individuals are better at leading in one capacity than in another.

Any sports fan can tell you only teams win championships. A collection of people pursuing individual goals is not a team.

SERVICE ENHANCEMENT

CHAPTER EIGHT

This Place Is A Zoo

Several years ago, the city of San Diego began a service enhancement program for its 16 different departments. Grants were made to departments which came up with the most promising proposals. I wandered about observing and interviewing the City Manager and other officials such as those in the Fire, Library, Property Management, Training, Finance, and Zoological departments to learn what they were doing. The Fire Department had found ways to make inspection of buildings more convenient for city property owners, businesses, and builders by simply changing its schedule to begin earlier and stay open later and by simplifying forms.

An information line was established to help the public learn whom to contact in case of a problem, something that Chicago could have used. Service enhancement in the city's nationally famous zoo was not just a short-time experiment. It was a commitment to better serve the millions of guests that swarm through its gates each year.

Service enhancement began with settling a backlog of union grievances and a concerted effort to improve employee working conditions. It started with a SPEAK UP FOR ACTION survey. Zoo management solicited ideas from employees and then set up teams to put these ideas into action. This evolved into trial projects for self-directed work groups charged with the complete management of bio-climatic zones.

I interviewed those working in the Tiger River Run. The Tiger River team managed its budget and cross-trained the animal and grounds keepers. The Tiger River team was charged with the design of, and decisions about, its display. Follow-up surveys showed that this long-term Speak-Up for Action program improved employee job satisfaction.

In another zoo, this one in Cleveland, the animal keepers complained that they were left out. They asked, why should management bring in volunteers to tell the public about the animals? "We know our animals best. We should be the ones telling the public about them," several of the animal keepers exclaimed. Here were workers frustrated because they were not allowed to get close to customers.

Getting Closer To The Public

At the Smithsonian, in addition to interviewing management, I observed guards who appeared quite bored. Eight hours a day, wandering from room to room, standing, mostly not even allowed to sit is tiring. Guards did not talk to the crowds about what was before them. "Why?" I asked them, could they not be trained in art history, aircraft history, or natural science history? Would they enjoy trading off with other guards, telling the crowds about their exhibits to break up the task of guarding? It was an idea they liked. Training the guards to speak to museum guests about the exhibits would enrich their jobs.

Service Enhancement

They then would be seen as human rather than as uniformed statues which one would pass by with averted eyes.

Because I have liked my stays in Westin Hotels, I studied their training and noted the attention given to

> *ATTITUDE & ACTION*
>
> The Mission Statement of the City of San Diego is printed on a business card that carries the city's seal and begins with the motto: IF THEY HAD A CHOICE, OUR CUSTOMERS WOULD CHOOSE US.
>
> Provide high-quality municipal services and facilities.
>
> Respond in an equitable, efficient, and effective manner to community needs.
>
> Innovate to continually improve the service we provide.
>
> Develop a well-planned community for residents, visitors and employees.
>
> Enhance the environment and improve the quality of life in San Diego.

employees using guests' names and to providing extra services such as arranging departures to airports. Service personnel, after correcting a complaint of a guest, were trained to call guests to learn if the problem had been resolved. Even for a short stay, it is the guests' positive relationship with the hotel personnel that results in scheduling their next stay in a Westin.

Customer-contact involves emotions. When customers suffer, they will find ways to get back at those who cause their pain. But customer contact can also be emotional work that pleasantly satisfies both the contact person and the customer. We have a business near us that prides itself in its name--Fussy Cleaners. Job candidates who despise attention to detail should not be employed by Fussy. We enjoy being "grandmother fussed-over" customers and our appreciation flows back to them because of the exceptional attention they give their cleaning.

Confidence Is Earned

Closeness to the customer does not come about over-night. Service businesses that pay so low that their help is ever on alert for a better paying job elsewhere are short-sighted. Underpaid employees can not see themselves as deliverers of success. They can not produce an instant-closeness to customers. Nor can customers feel close to or have confidence in a parade of new hires.

Service Enhancement

> ### ATTITUDE & ACTION
>
> The right to have accurate and adequate information upon which to make free and intellligent decisions--and to be protected against false and misleading claims.
>
> *--From The Consumers' Bill of Rights, U.S. Office of Cusumer Affairs*

Service must not be seen as a function--such as repairing a broken water pump, operating upon a clogged artery, taking a customer's order. The service relationship rather is a process, a linkage within a complex web of suppliers, makers of things, machine maintenance, office and billing, and of those who actually deliver a service. The quality of the relationship among all those involved in the complex process of delivering a service will determine customer closeness and confidence.

50,000 Moments Of Truth

Dan West, who formatted this book, came in steaming as I was working on this chapter. Dan had just come from a hardware store, the largest in our area. A day before he had purchased a bathroom wall fan for his condo which the sales person had told him would work in either a ceiling or wall. Upon reading the instructions at home, he learned he had bought a ceiling only fan. So he took the fan back to the hardware's exchange counter, and then went to the department from which he had purchased the wrong fan to find one appropriate for wall installation.

After a time, he returned to the exchange counter without a fan and told the individual in charge of the exchange counter, "I could not find a salesperson in the back by the fans. I guess you don't want to sell me a fan." The individual at the exchange desk promptly replied, "I guess not. So I'll just ring up a refund for you." Dan said that here was another real-life example for my book. "All she would have had to do is pick up a phone to call a salesperson," he said in disgust.

Dan's annoyance was just one of many ways employees coolly brush off customers. Such employees' attitude and actions almost scream, "If it weren't for these customers, I could get some work done and then get out of here." That same kind of attitude and behavior all too often is the message one employee sends to a co-worker, seemingly forgetting that co-workers are internal customers who serve outside customers. And so we hear the complaint about the difficulty of working with so and so, or that department, or the bureaucracy.

Jan Carlzon is credited with turning around debt-ridden Scandinavian Airlines System (SAS) to be the most punctual and preferred airline in Europe. Hugely in the black, SAS was named "airline of the year."

How came the turnaround? In addition to making SAS equipment and schedules business-friendly, all 20,000 SAS employees took a two day service-first training.

Carlzon's message was simple--no matter how remote any employee is from the customer, there are thousands of moments every day which either turn the customers off or on. "We have 50,000 moments of truth out here every day," he was fond of saying. No CEO or public relations department can manage so many moments when customer impressions are formed. That is a job for every employee every day.

> *ATTITUDE & ACTION*
>
> A moment of truth is an episode in which a customer comes in contact with a company representative who leaves a vivid impression to be remembered for a long time. If that meeting is pleasant, customer confidence will be enhanced.

Value-added is a matter of attitude and action for each of us as individuals, for the very competitive world of business, and for the not-for-profit sector so important to the quality of the life of every hamlet and city. Adding value, as I understand it, is a continuous effort to improve quality; it is integrity of products and service; it is character at work. Adding value is that unrelenting thirst for goodness. It is soul-work.

THE NEXT CHAPTER

CHAPTER NINE

The Next Chapter

WHY NOT A CIRCUS?

The golden age of the American circus dates back over one hundred years. In 1881, Phineas T. Barnum combined his show with James A. Bailey's that soon was advertised as The Greatest Show On Earth. In 1884, the five Ringling brothers started a rival show. Then in 1907, the Ringlings bought Barnum & Bailey Circus, and in 1919 brought them together under one tent. That's a short history of the circus you and I enjoy today in large stadiums and indoor coliseums.

So what does this have to do with you and me? You say that you will not run away and join the circus. Right?Ced Wrong. You may call the place you work a zoo, but in many ways, where most of us work would be more accurately called a circus. There are our clowns, jackasses, star performers, jugglers, and lion tamers. Even a poorly run circus, more so than a well run zoo such as San Diego's described in the previous chapter, takes skilled management, coordination of many departments, and a competent-committed work force. Several principles explain our "so what."

A circus performance is a fantastic display of talent and can-do. History does not reveal what goes on to make a circus happen--the recruitment of unusually skilled performers, costume makers, the dieticians and animal keepers, the roustabouts who set up and tear down the acts, vendors, advance men,

ATTITUDE & ACTION

National Geographic's photographers have caught animals at play--A polar bear juggles a tire near Churchill, Alaska. After besting a rival bear for this tire, the comedian polar bear draped it about his neck. On a schussable snowbank in Alaska's Denail National Park, a juvenile grizzly bear skids down on all fours. A high spirited young mountain goat jumps and twists in Montana's Glacier National Park. A sea lion pup in the Galapagos tosses an iguana about in a tide pool. A Japanese macaque embraces a snowball he has rolled. Adult Grevy zebras in Kenya playfully nip each other's ears. Psychiatrist Stewart Brown, who has studies wild animals at play and children deprived of play, says "Play is an important part of a healthy, happy childhood, and playful adults are often highly creative, even brilliant individuals." Could it be that those who work together will work better if they also play together? Might work be better where it is something like a circus?

--inspired by Stewart L. Brown in Animals At Play, National Geographic.

band, ticket takers, stage managers, personnel managers, purchasing managers, accountants and financial managers, and of course the ring-master. And there are others we never think of such as blacksmiths, cooks, veterinarians, mechanics, and even transportation managers who plan travel between cities by train and truck.

All the components I have addressed in this book must come together to make a circus. A can-do attitude springs from the strong character traits of courage, persistence, and effort. Our worth, I argue, is determined by our competence, conscientiousness, and what we can contribute to the place where we work. The success of the workplace may be judged upon the jobs it brings to a region and more importantly to that intangible human construction we know as community.

A circus' purpose is to add pleasure. Perhaps you, as I do, can remember the excitement of attending your first circus or more recently of taking your children. What a circus does is to change ordinary space into a place of wonderful entertainment. Its purpose is to bring laughter, amazement, and a light to the eyes. Workplace climate and culture are shaped by the jugglers of competence, commitment, and communication-richness. Clowning can make work more fun.

Here is an example. This CEO zips to work in her pickup truck. One day she showed up in a Mickey Mouse skirt to yank down the bigwigs's reserved parking signs. She insists that managers must delegate more if they cannot get themselves and their employees home in time for dinner.

Fifty international managers invited to a strategy meeting were not taken on Outward Bound team-building exercises of rock climbing or tennis ball tossing while blindfolded, but an official photo of the meeting shows them in neat rows, all properly attired and each wearing Groucho Marx glasses, nose and mustache. She has her dozen direct reports drop by her office every two or three weeks and encourages them to reward mistakes. On a video introducing a new management incentive plan, she said, "I'm 47 years old and I don't get excited anymore about very much. But let me tell you, I am excited about the new W.H. Brady Management Incentive Plan..."

Katherine Hudson, Chief Executive Officer of W.H. Brady, a Milwaukee based manufacturer of floppy disk parts, radiation-hazard signs, and 30,000 other products, is a mover and shaker. Fun-making is part of her team management style. When she was the top woman manager at Kodak, she gave gold-plated crabgrass cutters to employees who rooted out useless procedures. Once to make the point to her staff that times were tough, she served generic beer and pretzels. To liven meetings up, sometimes she brought a stuffed gorilla named Seymour.

A circus is a critical mass of connectedness, coordination and roustabout cooperation. Henry Ringling North, when he was vice president of the Ringling Brothers and Barnum & Bailey Circus, said that "Circus people work together like members of a huge family." Often even the stars of the show perform in acts beside their own, or help with everyday chores.

Today's competition for world-class goods and service demands a circus kind of connectedness and cooperation. Capital investment in technology and intellectual talent are wasted unless coordinated. Cooperation and coordination hinge upon motivations often ignored by management--the aspirational achievement motives of mission and meaningful work and the relational motives of connectedness.

This chain of reasoning finds good purpose and meaningful work rooted in moral values. By that we mean doing what makes where we live liveable, contributes to community well-being, and protects the environment.

The survival of the circus hinges upon its individual and collective commitment to continuous quality improvement. Quality is a word that sums up meaningful work and continuous quality improvement refers to the complex process that must be system-wide to make it happen. Continuous quality improvement, if it is to be more than a passing corporate fad, must be manifest in individuals learning new skills and cultivation of virtue.

The success of a circus turns upon partnership. Loyalty can not be one-way if an organization is to succeed. Employees must commit to work as if they owned the workplace and employers must commit themselves to their employees. For optimal coordination and cooperation, workers' voice should be encouraged. Voice is evident in employee involvement, job enrichment, cooperation rather than adversarial management-labor relations, and self-managed teams. Traditional work for pay is not a sufficient condition for organization-wide continuous quality effort. The rewards of work must be fairly distributed; in the for-profit sector that entails gain-and profit sharing, and employee stock ownership.

Supplier-customer relationships work best when conceived of as partnering. Inside a workplace, the interdependence of departments is best understood as an internal supplier-customer partnership. Confidence in supply and delivery turns upon developing close supplier relations.

Satisfying the ultimate customer also turns upon developing a close relationship. Companies that are most successful solicit input in the design of products and delivery of services. Customer-contact workers are selected because they are nice people. In as much as possible, production workers should interact with their front-line customer-contact workers. Not just satisfaction, but **customer confidence** is the goal of a provider. A circus must cultivate a partnership with any venue in which it expects a return engagement.

If Not A Circus, Why Not Butterflies?

Now to end this book on an even lighter note than joining the circus. In the community in which I live, recently retired Sara Troop is known for raising monarch butterflies. For years, she has nurtured this hobby in addition to her job at a nearby university of teaching teachers how to teach children reading.

The Next Chapter

According to Troop, monarch butterflies come from pin size eggs laid on the underside of milkweed leaves that hatch into caterpillars. Within two weeks these caterpillars, feeding upon the milkweed, increase to more than 2,700 times their original weight. A collection of eggs on milkweed soon transform her porch into a butterfly haven. They also transform the homes of children to whom she has given many a caterpillar. Following this hobby, has taken her to Mexico, 9,000 feet up a remote mountain where the monarchs from the eastern part of north America winter after crossing the Gulf of Mexico.

The point here is to conclude by asking what are you and I doing that excites us, if not on the job, then as an avocation? What are we doing to add value to where we live and work? If not butterflies, what?

In this book, I have done my bit to add value to you my readers. Now I am history as far as you are concerned. It is up to you to write the next chapter--your chapter.

References

A Cat Fight With No Winners. Business Week. 104.

Albrecht, Karl, & Zemke, Ron. (1985). Service America: Doing Business in the New Economy. Homewood, IL: Dow Jones-Irwin.

Barnet, Richard J. (1994, December 19). Lords of the Global Economy. The Nation. 754-757.

Bemowski, Karen. (1994, October). Ford Chairman Was, and Continues To Be, a Progress Chaser. Quality Progress. 29-32.

Benneyan, Jim. (1994, July). Executive Summary. Quality Progress. 23.

Bernstein, Aaron. (1994, August 14). Inequality: How the Gap Between Rich and Poor Hurts The Economy. Business Week, 78-83.

Bernstein, Aaron. (1994, May 23). Why America Needs Unions But Not The Kind It Has Now. Business Week, 70-82.

Berton, Lee. (1994, October 11). Ernst & Young Decimates Its Legal Department. The Wall Street Journal. B1.

Bok, Derek. (1993). The Cost of Talent: How Executives and Professionals Are Paid and How It Affects America. New York: Free Press.

Cheser, Raymond. (1994, April). Kaizen Is More Than Continuous Improvement. Quality Progress. 23-25.

Christison, William L. (1994, July). Financial Information Is Key to

Clair, Robin. (1993). The Use of Framing Devices To Sequester Organizational Narratives: Hegemony and Harassment. Communication Monographs, 113-136.

Corn, David. (1994, October 10). C.I.A. vs. F.O.I.A. The Nation. 369-370. Empowerment. Quality Progress. 47-48.

Davis, Stan, & Botkin, Jim. (1994). The Monster Under The Bed: How Business Is Mastering The Opportunity Of Knowledge For Profit. New York: Simon & Schuster.

Dumaine, Brian. (1994, September 5). The Trouble With Teams. Fortune. 86-92.

Dumaine, Brian. (1994, December 26). Why Do We Work? Fortune. 196-200.

Earhart, Amelia. (1932). The Fun Of It. New York: Brewer, Warren & Putnam.

Evans, Dianne. (1994, June 17). It's A Brave New World At Telxon. The Akron Beacon Journal, B8.

Evans-Correia, K. (1990, August 16). Office Temporaries. Purchasing. 96-99.

Fierman, Jaclyn. (1994, June 13). The Perilous New World of Fair Pay. Fortune, 57-64.

Freeman, Richard B., Ed. (1994). Working Under Different Rules. New York: Russell Sage Foundation.

General Motors Environmental Report. (1994). Detroit, MI: General Motors Corporation.

Gorden, William & Nevins, Randi. (1993). We Mean Business. New York: Harper Collins.

Graves, Jacqueline M. (1994, May 30). Management Tools That Work. Fortune, 26.

Greising, David. (1994, August 8). Quality: How To Make It Pay. Business Week, 54-59.

Graves, Jacqueline M. (1994, May 30). Management Tools That Work. Fortune. 30.

Grover, Ronald, Bernstein, Aaron, & Schiller, Zachary. (1994, August 15). Top Of The News: Labor. Business Week, 26-28.

Guide To The Global 500. (1994, July 25). Fortune. 137-190.

Hamel, Gary & Prahalad, C. K. (1994, September 5). Seeing the Future First. Fortune. 64-70.

Harbrect, Douglas. (1994, July 11). Talk About Murder Inc. Business Week, 8.

Henkoff, Ronald. (1994, June 27). Service Is Everybody's Business. Fortune, 48-60.

Herrnstein, Richard J. & Murray, Charles. (1994). The Bell Curve: Intelligence and Class Structure In America. New York: The Free Press.

Hilgart, Art. (1994, November 21). The U.Q. Test For Success. Nation. 614.

Howe, Roger J., Gaeddert, Dee & Howe, Maynard A. (1992). Quality On Trial. St. Paul: West Publishing.

Huey, John. (1994, May 30) The Absolute Best Way To Fly. Fortune, 128.

Impoco, Jim. (1994, August 8). Sliding Toward A Strike. U.S. News & World Report, 49.

Is the Baldrige Overblown? (1991, July 1). Fortune.

Johnson, Susan & Marano, Hara E. (1994, March/April). Love: The Immutable Longing for Contact. Psychology Today, 32-37.

Kelly, Kevin. (1994, May 16). Cat Is Purring, But They're Hissing On The Floor. Business Week, 33.

Kelly, Kevin. (1994, November 7). The Drought Is Over At 3M. Business Week. 140-141.

References

Kelley, Kevin, Woodruff, David & Bernstein, Aaron. (1994, July 4). Much Ado About Pettiness. Business Week, 34-36.

King, Sarah, S. & Cushman, Donald, P. (1994, November). High-speed Management and Organizational Communication: Cushman and King Associates. Paper presented at the Speech Communication Association Convention, New Orleans.

Koretz, Gene. (1994, August 15). Profit-Sharing Gooses Productivity--For A While. Business Week, 22.

Kuper, Andrew. (1995, January 16). A "Whole New Medium" Online. Fortune. 16.

Labich, Kenneth. (1994, November 14). Why Companies Fail. Fortune. 52-68.

Loeb, Marshall. (1995, January 16). Ten Commandments For Managing Creative People. Fortune. 135-136.

Logan, Todd. (1995, January). Mind of the Manager: Trapped. INC. 21-22.

Lublin, Joann S. (1994, October 3). It's Shape-Up Time for Performance Review. The Wall Street Journal. B1-B2.

Mamis, Robert A. (1994, June). Partner Wars. INC., 36-44.

Management Practices: U.S. Companies Improve Performance Through Quality Efforts. United States General Accounting Office, GAO/NSIAD-91-190. May, 1991.

McCullough, David. (1992). Truman. New York: Touchstone.

Mitchell, Russell, & Oneal, Michael. (1994, August 1). Managing By Values: Is Levi Strauss' Approach Visionary--or Flaky? Business Week, 46-52.

Mitchell, Russell. (1994, August 1). Managing By Values. Business Week, 46-52.

Nasar, Sylvia. (1994, June). America's Free Market: The Global Winner. Reader's Digest, 114-116. Condensed from The New York Times, February 27, 1994.

Norton, Rob. (1994, November 28). New Thinking On The Causes--And Costs--Of Yes Men (And Women). Fortune. 31.

O'Reilly, Brian. (1994, June 13). The New Deal: What Companies and Employees Owe One Another. Fortune, 44-52.

O'Reilly, Brian. (1994, October 17). 360 Feedback Can Change Your Life. Fortune. 30-100.

Our Story So Far: Notes from the first 75 years of 3M Company. (1977). St. Paul, Minnesota: Minnesota Mining and Manufacturing Company.

Overman, S. (1993, August). Temporary Services Go Global. Human Resources Management. 72-74.

Partnership Handbook: A Roadmap Partnership. (1994). Washington DC: National Partnership Clearinghouse.

Patterson, Jack. (1994, October 17). The New World Of Work. Business Week. 76-87.

Persico, John & McLean, Gary N. (1994, April). Manage With Valid Rather Than Invalid Goals. Quality Progress, 49-53.

Peters, Tom. (1992). Liberation Management: Necessary Disorganization for the Nanosecond Nineties. New York: Fawcett Columbine.

Reich, Robert B. (1995, February). Letters: Class Anxious. Harpers. 4-5.

Reynolds, L. (1994). Washington Confronts Part-time America. Management Review. 83, 27-28.

Rich, Doris L. (1989). Amelia Earhart. The Smithsonian Institution.

Rigdon, Joan E. (1994, September 29). Some Workers Gripe Bosses Are Ordering Too Much Overtime. The Wall Street Journal. A1.

Samuelson, Robert J. (1994, April 25). The More and Less Deserving Rich. Newsweek, 43.

Serling, Robert J. (1992). The Story of Boeing and Its People: Legend and Legacy. New York: St. Martin's Press.

Serwer, Andrew E. (1994, October 17). McDonald's Conquer's The World. Fortune. 103-116.

Shellenbarger, Sue. (1994, October 12). Child-Care Crunch Puts Parents Between The Kids and The Boss. The Wall Street Journal. B1.

Sherman, Straford. (1994, August 22). Leaders Learn To Heed The Voice Within. Fortune, 92-100.

Smith, Bradford, A. (1994, January). New Eyes on the Universe. National Geographic, 2-41.

Smith, Lee. (1994, July 25). Burned-out Bosses. Fortune. 44-52.

Smith, Ruth & Eisenberg, Eric. (1985). Conflict and the Co-optation of Root-Metaphors at Disneyland. Paper presented at the Speech Communication Association, Denver.

Smith, Timothy, K. (1994, December 12). What's So Effective about Stephen Covey? Fortune. 116-126.

Steeples, Marion M. (1994, June). The Quality-Ethics Connection. Quality Progress, 73-75.

Stewart, Thomas A. (1994, October 3). Your Company's Most Valuable Asset: Intellectual Capital. Fortune. 68-70.

Stewart, Thomas A. (1994, November 28). How To Lead A Revolution. Fortune. 48-61.

Taylor, Alex. (1994, September 5). The Auto Industry Meets The New Economy. Fortune. 52-60.

References

Taylor, Alex. (1994, October 17). GM's $11,000,000,000 Turnaround. Fortune. 54-74.

Teerlink, Rich. (1994, August 22). Now Hear This. Fortune, 20.

Teresa Harris v. Forklift Systems Inc. (1993). 62 U.S.L.W. 4004.

The New American Workplace: A Labor Perspective. (1994). Washington, DC: AFL-CIO.

Thurow, Lester. (1992). Head To Head: The Coming Economic Battle Among Japan, Europe, and America. New York: William Morrow.

Treece, James B., Shiller, Zachary, & Kelly, Kevin. (1994, August 8). Hardball Is Still GM's Game. Business Week. 26.

Trujillo, Nick. (1992). Interpreting (the Work and the Talk of) Baseball: Perspectives on Ballpark Culture. Western Journal of Communication, 350-371.

Vonada, Damaine. (1994, November). The Fifth Horseman. Ohio Magazine. 35-44, 129-135.

Williams, Michael. (1994, October 24). Back to the Past: Some Plants Tear Out Long Assembly Lines, Switch to Craft Work. The Wall Street Journal. A1, A4.

Whitney, John. (1994). The Trust Factor: Liberating Profits and Restoring Corporate Vitality. New York: McGraw.

Value Added Attitude And Action

The list of organizations and work-sites where I've trained, consulted, toured and/or interviewed employees about quality for this book is extensive:

Abbott Laboratories, Akron General Metropolitan Hospital, Allen Bradley, American Greetings, American Society for Quality Control, Arthur Anderson, Boeing, Boy Scouts of America, CNN, CBS, NBC, Disney, Centerior Energy, Cleveland Metropolitan Park, Cleveland School System, D.C. Coalition for the Homeless, RR Donnelley, Coors, Copperweld Steel, Crosby Quality College, FANNIMAE, Firestone-Bridgestone, Food Lion, Friendly's, General Dynamics, General Electric, General Motors, Girl Scouts of America, B.F. Goodrich, Goodyear, Harley Davidson, Hilton Hotels, Hoecht Celenese, IRS, Labor Department, Merck, 3MM, McDonald's, Merrill Lynch, Navy, Motorola, NASA, Northwestern Mutual Life, NCR, Parker-Hannefin, Procter & Gamble, Rockwell, San Diego City government, (Manager, Finance, Fire, Library, Propoerty Management Departments, and zoo), Sears, Sheraton Hotels, Shoney's, Stouffers' Foods, The Smithsonian, Social Security, Timken, Union Carbide, U.S. Postal Service, US-Kolbe Steel, United Van Lines, United Way, Westinghouse, WLR Foods, Xerox, etc.

This list does not include a number of hospitals, professional organizations, and small companies.

About The Author

For the past twenty years, William I. Gorden has specialized in organizational communication studies. With his colleague and good friend Dominic Infante, he has investigated the boss-bossed relationship.
From coast to coast and abroad in Europe and the Far East, Bill Gorden has wandered about observing, talking to people about their jobs. He has done the same kind of wandering through thousands of business periodicals and books.
Bill earned the M.S. and Ph.D at Purdue and did postdoctoral study at Northwestern and Florida State universities. He has served on the faculty of Purdue, Berry College, Southwest Texas State University, Kent State University, and was a visiting professor at Luven University in Belgium.
Dr. Gorden has written: <u>Nine Men Plus</u>, <u>Communication Personal and Public</u>, and <u>Time Capsules</u> and co-authored several others including <u>Team Dynamics In Developing Organizations</u>, <u>Employee Values in a Changing Society</u>, and <u>We Mean Business</u> published by Harper Collins.
He has done extensive training and consultation work with several major corporations: assisted in a two year organizational development program with a Fortune 500 manufacturing company, trained a twenty-person speakers' bureau for a steel company, did executive presentation training for a lawn care company, and instructed a tire-safety engineer in

delivery of trial testimony in a six-million dollar wrongful death suit.

Bill has teamed with Dr. John Miller in much of his training and consultation. They have done a series of one to two day training sessions on topics of communication and motivation for several associations such as the International Management Clubs and the National Association of Secretaries. These usually involved numbers from 40-500 persons and took the pair from Augusta, Georgia to far away places such as Hilo, Hawaii.

More recently, Gorden and Miller, over a year and one half, conducted nine weeks of team-building training for a General Electric plant. Training was scheduled for 20 to 40 employees (a mix of line, staff, and managers) on all three shifts until the total plant had participated. After that, they made a 20 minute video production describing that team-building effort.

Gorden and Miller have also co-authored the books Speak Up For Business, Managing Your Communication: In And For The Organization, and Working For The Best Can Jump Start America.